Criterion-Referenced Testing for the Social Studies

Paul L. Williams
and Jerry R. Moore,
Editors

National Council for the Social Studies • Bulletin 64

ABOUT THE EDITORS

PAUL L. WILLIAMS is Chief, Program Assessment, Evaluation, and Instructional Support, Maryland State Department of Education. He is responsible for the development and implementation of the state testing programs.

JERRY R. MOORE is Professor of Education at the University of Virginia. He served as Chairperson of the Department of Curriculum and Instruction from 1971 to 1977.

Library of Congress Catalog Card Number: 80-848-89
ISBN 0-87986-034-0
Copyright © 1980 by the
NATIONAL COUNCIL FOR THE SOCIAL STUDIES
3615 Wisconsin Ave., N.W., Washington, D.C. 20016

Contents

Cover Design by Henriet Brigada

Foreword

Elaine Lindheim begins her chapter in this Bulletin with these words:

Tests have been around almost as long as there have been teachers, and there are probably as many different kinds of tests as there are instructors. There are hard tests, easy tests, long tests, short tests, multiple-choice tests, essay tests, cognitive tests, affective tests, individual tests, group tests, placement tests, diagnostic tests, nationally-produced tests, and locally-devised tests.

I am sure that, if pressed to do so, Ms. Lindheim could go on and on. Certainly, to this multifaceted picture of testing, there is one more approach that must be added—criterion-referenced testing, which continues to receive the serious and intensive attention of educators throughout the nation.

It is particularly timely, therefore, that this NCSS Bulletin focuses upon this important area of testing. Thoughtfully written chapters of the book discuss current issues and practices in social studies assessment, ways to improve testing, and methodologies to strengthen the validity, reliability, and value of tests; and a brief bibliography of social studies tests provides the reader with additional useful information. The Bulletin thus succeeds in its primary purpose of bringing the social studies profession up to date about the issues and strategies involving criterion-referenced testing.

On behalf of the National Council for the Social Studies, I wish to express appreciation to the editors, Paul L. Williams and Jerry R. Moore, and to the chapter authors for their contribution to the publications program of our organization and to our profession.

Todd Clark, *President*
National Council for the Social Studies

1

Social Studies Testing: Current Issues

Jerry R. Moore and Paul L. Williams

Social studies education has been recently characterized as that instructional area where little significant research on teacher education and student outcomes has been produced (Smith, 1979). Smith has referred to research knowledge about social studies as "meagre and friable." Assuming the accuracy of this statement, the determination of instructional objectives and the assessment of student performances in the social studies have been difficult.

Social studies educators have consistently written about an appropriate process for curriculum/instruction development (Taba). This theoretical, traditional model of curriculum development can be characterized as follows:

Defining the Social Studies
(Philosophy/Rationale)
↓
Describing Curriculum Goals
↓
Determining Instructional Objectives
↓
Planning Instruction
↓
Assessing Student Performances

A major problem in utilizing the model is that there is considerable confusion in the profession about almost every one of its processes. Issues in defining the social studies have been effectively treated by Barr, Barth, and Shermis (1978). Their portrayal of definitional issues clearly demonstrates conflictual elements in the social studies that confront the curriculum developer.

The fact that there are differing definitions for the social studies need not be debilitating in curriculum development. It can be, and often is, argued that diversity and conflict are essential elements of the social studies profession; and that these elements contribute to expanded thinking about the social studies and consequently result in professional growth. With the exception of a few select social studies educators, social studies professionals have not provided much help in focusing or clearing up the definitional crisis. The *NCSS Curriculum Guidelines* (1971/1976), the subject of discussion in Chapter 2, reflect this confusion in specifying curriculum goals.

Unfortunately, social studies educators rarely present analyses that illustrate how curriculum choices have an impact upon instructional objectives and assessment (one notable exception is Oliver and Shaver, 1966). Consequently, locally produced rationales and curriculum goals tend to accommodate "all" definitions of the social studies. As a result, curricular ambiguity abounds, interfering with instructional success and making the "targeting" of assessment difficult, or even impossible.

The subject of this Bulletin, therefore, is more precisely focused upon the need to clarify and to understand the issues related to the delineation of social studies outcomes within the processes of assessment, particularly criterion-referenced assessment. A cursory examination of social studies "methods" textbooks and literature illustrates the problem of how a lack of delineation may have an adverse impact on clear assessment. Suggested social studies outcomes might include (Samford and Cottle, 1952):

> to gain unbounded enthusiasm for the ideals of democracy as a form of government. (p. 10)

or confusing outcomes, as reported in *The Social Studies Professional,* (1980):

> A. Social Studies Purpose I: Education for citizenship in a democratic state and global society.
> 1. Career Education Skill: Skills in basic understanding and appreciation of the private enterprise system. . . . (p. 1)

Assessment of these or similar objectives is impossible since the level of description is at best inadequate for instructional planning or feedback through measurement. How can anyone determine "unbounded enthusiasm" or skills related to "appreciation" unless they are unambiguously described?

Similarly, social studies literature has contained eloquent, if not very specific, discussions of measurement and evaluation—discussions that suggest that the purposes of evaluation include: (1) sorting, ranking, and grading individuals within groups; (2) diagnosing student needs and prescribing instructional behaviors; and (3) certifying the promotion and graduation of individuals. Far too often these discussions have been cosmetic and incomplete. Most "methods" texts, for example, offer the reader a smorgasbord of goals for inclusion in the social studies curriculum; a discussion of the multicontent bases for social studies instruction; and a simplistic, generalized description of assessment processes. The processes and purposes of assessment are seldom, if ever, linked to the discussions of the various objectives. What the "methods" texts do include are comments on the qualities of various test items, the differing types of objective tests, the qualities of the essay test, and some less formal assessments of student performance. In addition, the textbook writers typically suggest that social studies tests should provide for the diagnosis of individual student performances either through pretest/posttest analysis or through formative evaluation, as well as providing information for the grading and/or sorting of students. What is glaringly absent are discussions of the processes necessary to achieve those goals.

Inadequate treatment of assessment issues in social studies has been a longstanding condition. The general appraisal of testing in Charles Beard's *Conclusions and Recommendations* (1934) is illustrative of difficulties in resolving assessment questions:

> 1. The assumption that new-type (objective) tests can guide and measure the efficiency of instruction in the social sciences is based on misconceptions of social processes, and such tests, except where used as occasional checks on other examining methods, do positive damage to the minds and powers of children in the ways already indicated. (p. 100)

The Beard commission recognized the obvious misfit between existing tests and their goals for instruction, but it was unwilling or unable to examine ways in which the science of testing could be improved to match loftier purposes, or to address ways in which loftier purposes could be directed for more precise measurement. It is possible that a similar situation exists today. For example, the excellent book *Social Studies for Our Times* (Gross, et al., 1978) may be illustrative of this situation. Of twenty-three chapters in this book, fifteen attend to the analyses of the social studies, while only one chapter is devoted to assessment. Furthermore, the chapters on the sources of the social studies include three chapters on the definition of social studies, four chapters on the social studies and the social sciences, seven chapters on methods and inquiry, and, finally, eight chapters on new foci in social studies—e.g., careers, consumerism. The linkage between curriculum goals, instructional outcomes, and assessment was theorized without attending to operational implications.

The limited number of articles in *Social Education* concerning student assessment reflects a similar gap. One which has appeared incorrectly implies that advocates of criterion-referenced measurement claim that criterion-referenced tests *per se* result in increased student achievement (Wehlage, Popkewitz, and Hartoonian, 1973). The article argues that criterion-referenced tests

> . . . employ assumptions about knowledge that are inconsistent with the scholarship of the social disciplines and the realities of the modern world. (p. 768)

The problem with this statement is obvious. It is the professionals who are charged with defining test content who may not understand the "realities of the modern world."

This is not to argue that NCSS publications have completely ignored assessment. The November–December, 1976, issue of *Social Education* is an excellent source for the construction of classroom tests. NCSS Bulletins by Anderson and Lindquist (1960, 1964) and Morse and McCune (1964) contain sample test items for World History and American History and study skills, respectively. These Bulletins, in addition to providing teachers with a selection pool of test items for classroom use, suggest ideas for the construction of classroom tests. While these Bulletins have been extremely helpful to teachers in preparing test items, the relationships between the items and actual instructional objectives for a given classroom were dependent upon the teachers' ability to describe appropriate criteria for selecting items. Emphasis throughout was upon the quality of the item for itself, rather than upon the match between test items and the intended learning outcomes, where the outcomes have been sufficiently described. Without any clear description, virtually no match is assured.

Evaluation in Social Studies (the Thirty-fifth Yearbook of the NCSS) has been another extremely valuable work for the improvement of testing practices in the social studies classroom. The Yearbook is an excellent resource on ideas about testing in the social studies, alternative forms of testing, and special concepts of measurement often ignored within the profession. What this and most other social studies publications have not attempted to explain is how the social studies teacher (educator) must (can) carefully describe the social studies outcomes in ways that provide criteria for the preparation of test items and the adequate targeting of instruction consistent with them. They have not confronted or explicated issues of relative versus absolute standards of student performance, of criterion-referenced versus norm-referenced measurement.

William Hartley's preface to the Thirty-Fifth Yearbook asserted that "the process of testing in the social studies has long been a problem area—the subject of disagreement and controversy." His statement of fifteen years ago is still timely. As previously documented, the clear specification of student outcomes, and a coherent, systematic approach to verifying student acquisition of the outcomes, have not yet come to the social studies. Compounding this situation are the current demands and pressures upon the educational community, of which social studies is a part, that could not have been foreseen at the time the 1965 Yearbook was published. These demands and pressures have been manifested in the form of the accountability movement. Associated with the accountability thrust are requirements that students demonstrate, usually through some form of testing, the "mastery" of outcomes deemed important: worthiness for promotion, and/or eligibility for high school graduation. Testing strategies proposed and used in the past are not ideally suited for many of the purposes which presently characterize programs that attempt to certify student competency. *It is the primary purpose of this Bulletin to bring the social studies profession up to date about the issues and strategies related to testing designed for certification.*

The content of this Bulletin is not limited in its usefulness to states or districts currently involved in competency-based programs. As developed in subsequent chapters, the particular approach to testing advocated both here and in the recent *NCSS Position Statement on Graduation Competency Testing in the Social Studies* (Fox, Williams, and Winters, 1979) has significant implications for the measurement of student outcomes in the social studies generally. Perhaps the most singularly important characteristic of this approach— i.e., criterion-referenced testing—is that the outcomes to be tested must be clearly defined and described. This clear definition and description of student outcomes has been conspicuously absent from the literature related to the testing and evaluation of students in the social studies. In many instances, the outcomes have been well defined and described in the more prominent methods texts; but rarely have they been operationalized into a systematic descriptive scheme which would allow meaningful interpretations of student performances relative to outcomes of interest. For example, the book by Hunt and Metcalf (1968) provides an outstanding explanation of reflective thinking and teaching reflective thinking, but the authors do not provide a schema for assessing student proficiencies against intended outcomes.

The point of view expressed by Wehlage, Popkewitz, and Hartoonian (1973) that it is somehow improper to specify student outcomes within the context of an assessment program has been totally rejected in this Bulletin. It is through the unambiguous identification of outcomes, within the context of the assessment component of the classical curriculum model, that instruction can be planned and executed. This position does not imply that *all* outcomes can be quantified into paper-and-pencil performances. Nor does it imply that instruction should be narrowed in breadth and scope for the singular purpose of improving student test performance. What it does imply is that outcomes can and should be better described and defined, and that assessment should be consistent with intended learnings.

Can coherent assessment proceed if intended learnings, as contained in curricular documents, are unclear? Possibly. Unclear goals may be clarified through well defined criterion-referenced testing procedures; for by its very nature, criterion-referenced measurement requires clear descriptions of outcomes. In 1960 Howard Cummings hinted at this phenomenon:

> In the long run, the goals and objectives for the pupils in any social studies classroom tend to be whatever questions the teacher asks on his tests. These questions should be closely related to the list of objectives which have been built up and clarified by a generation of curriculum makers. . . . (p. v)

Thus, an iterative process could result where test outcomes are defined; curricula are then clarified, which in turn modifies test outcomes. This is a positive instance of what is termed "curriculum deflection"; e.g., modifying and directing instruction to reflect tested outcomes. Curriculum deflection, however, can also be seen in a pejorative sense. If tests reflect only a limited number of overly simplistic outcomes, and an inordinate amount of instructional effort is targeted toward them, then the test becomes the curriculum. Essentially, the minimums can become the maximums.

The development of high quality criterion-referenced measures can begin to establish a closer link than ever before between measurement and instruction. Indeed, more than a simple link is established; rather, a symbiotic relationship is forged that makes measurement and instruction equal partners in the teaching/learning process. The current state of the art of assessment in social studies would suggest that this relationship is not present. This situation carries with it the danger that classroom teachers may be diagnosing and prescribing for student needs from improper information, may be making claims for instruction that are inappropriate and irresponsible, and may be modifying curriculum goals and instructional plans on the basis of inconsistent data. Improvement of this condition is particularly important in situations where the results of assessment are intended to be used to diagnose student strengths and weaknesses and subsequently to remediate student deficiencies. The clear mandate in these situations is to use assessment results to improve instruction; i.e., to make instructional intervention as efficacious as possible. It is hoped that this Bulletin will be a contribution to the resolution of these issues.

In the chapters which follow, criterion-referenced measurement is discussed from several perspectives. Chapter 2 provides a review of recent NCSS activities in the area of testing. These activities include analyses of the *NCSS Curriculum Guidelines* (1971/1976) relative to nationally published social studies tests and trends in testing among the states within the accountability movement. One of the most striking features of the chapter is the documentation of the widespread implementation of accountability programs in the social studies. The testing component associated with such programs is one which invariably has as two of its purposes the certification function (promotion, graduation, etc.) and the instructional intervention function (diagnosis, remediation). The stage is thus set in Chapter 2 for the remaining chapters, where, consistent with the purposes for testing in accountability programs, criterion-referenced measurement is examined in some detail. As the data in Chapter 2 are considered, it should be kept in mind that the accountability movement is quite volatile nationally; and, while the data were accurate at the time they were collected, legislative mandates and action by state boards of education may have caused the information to become dated. While the chapter contains suggestions that criterion-referenced tests are being used in the testing components of accountability programs, the data are based on responses from educators with varying degrees of expertise in testing. It is possible—even likely—that some respondents have given less than accurate descriptions of their use of criterion-referenced testing.

The introduction of criterion-referenced measurement into the social studies is a new phenomenon. It is not surprising and quite understandable that many social studies professionals are not really sure about what it is. Chapter 3 presents a brief introduction to and definition of criterion-referenced measurement. The important characteristics of criterion-referenced tests (CRTs) are explained and are contrasted with norm-referenced and objectives-referenced tests. Perhaps one of the most significant contributions of the chapter is to show the feasibility of actually beginning to define and describe social studies outcomes in an unambiguous fashion through use of test specifications. Chapter 4 extends those ideas introduced in Chapter 3 by applying them in a school setting.

Chapter 5 analyzes one of the most popular social studies assessment approaches, the National Assessment of Educational Progress model, for its efficacy relative to individual student diagnosis and remediation. The issue of whether the NAEP model is appropriate for such interpretations is examined in some detail. Important considerations about the necessity of matching proper measurement processes with intended purposes for measurement are raised and discussed.

Procedures for ensuring a basic level of psychometric integrity for criterion-referenced tests (CRTs) are presented in Chapter 6. These procedures include methods for documenting the validity and relia- bility of either locally or externally developed CRTs. Preliminary concerns for constructing alternate test forms of equivalent diffi- culty and for setting cut-scores are also discussed. Most of the pro- cedures in Chapter 6 have been presented in a fashion that does not require a background in statistics or advanced measurement, nor do they require the use of computers.

Appendix I contains a brief bibliography of social studies tests, and Appendix II presents statistical data for Chapter 6.

REFERENCES

Anderson, H.R., and Lindquist, E.F. *Selected Test Items in American His- tory.* Bulletin 6. Washington, D.C.: National Council for the Social Stud- ies, 1964.

Anderson, H.R., and Lindquist, E.R. *Selected Test Items in World History.* Bulletin 9. Washington, D.C.: National Council for the Social Studies, 1960.

Barr, R.D., Barth, J.L., and Shermis, S.S. *Defining the Social Studies.* Bul- letin 51. Washington, D.C.: National Council for the Social Studies, 1977.

Beard, C.A. (et al.). *Conclusions and Recommendations of the Commission.* New York: Charles Scribner's Sons, 1934.

Berg, H.D. (Ed.). *Evaluation in Social Studies.* Thirty-fifth Yearbook. Washington, D.C.: National Council for the Social Studies, 1965.

Brown, L.B. (Ed.). *Social Education, 40,* November–December, 1976.

Fox, K.F.A., Williams, P.L., and Winters, L. "Graduation Competency Testing in the Social Studies: A Position Statement of the National Council for the Social Studies." In *Social Education, 43,* May, 1979, 367–372.

Gross, R.E., Messick, R., Chapin, J.R., and Sutherland, J. *Social Studies for Our Times.* New York: John Wiley and Sons, 1978.

Hoyt, K.B. "Social Studies Educators Urged to Emphasize 'Career Skills'." In *The Social Studies Professional,* February, 1980, 53.

Hunt, M.P., and Metcalf, L. *Teaching High School Social Studies.* New York: Harper and Row, 1968.

Morse, H.T., and McCune, G.H. *Selected Items for the Testing of Study Skills and Critical Thinking.* Bulletin 15. Washington, D.C.: National Council for the Social Studies, 1964.

Oliver, D., and Shaver, J.P. *Teaching Public Issues in the High School.* Bos- ton: Houghton Mifflin, 1966.

Samford, C.D., and Cottle, E. *Social Studies in the Secondary School.* New York: McGraw-Hill Book Company, Inc., 1952.

Smith, B.P. Research in Teacher Education. (Unpublished paper.)

Wehlage, G.G., Popkewitz, T.S., and Hartoonian, H.M. "Social Inquiry, Schools, and State Assessment." In *Social Education,* December, 1973, 766–770.

2

Social Studies Assessment: Current Practice

Jerry R. Moore

During 1977, Anna Ochoa, then President of the National Council for the Social Studies, established a Committee on Testing (COT) to undertake a study of testing practices in social studies education.[1] This chapter is a presentation of the procedures, findings, and conclusions of the COT studies.

PROCEDURES

Essentially, the COT was given the charge to:

Task 1: Derive classes of learning outcomes based upon the *NCSS Curriculum Guidelines* (1971) and the *NCSS Curriculum Guidelines for Multiethnic Education* (1976).

Task 2: Acquire a representative sample of commercially produced social studies tests and analyze these tests for congruency with learning outcomes derived from the *Guidelines.*[2]

Preliminary attempts to derive learning outcomes from the *Guidelines* produced serious concerns. The committee recognized that the *Guidelines* had been written by a committee of social studies educators representing the organizational diversity of the NCSS and were influenced by the prominent political and professional issues of that time. The COT further realized that the *Guidelines* were never intended as a basis for the identification of learning outcomes. Nevertheless, the *Guidelines* documents (1971/1976) contained checklist statements that were proposed for use in evaluating local social studies programs.

The COT solicited the help of social studies professionals representing classroom teachers and college educators.[3] These people rated each of the checklist statements contained in the *Guidelines* regarding its appropriateness for large-scale assessment. Since the checklists had been suggested as useful for program evaluation, it was assumed that the checklists were an accurate reflection of the larger body of the *Guidelines*.

The COT compiled the reports of the independent raters, using their ratings as a quasi-control on the subjectivity of the committee. The committee examined and discussed each guideline statement against two questions:

- *What is the intended learning outcome of the statement?*
- *Can the learning outcome be assessed through large-scale procedures?*

These deliberations and the rater reports produced a regrouping of the individual guidelines under the following categories:

Appropriate for National Assessment
Appropriate for Statewide Assessment
Appropriate for Local Assessment—Unobtrusive Measures
                                     —Attitudinal Measures
                                     —Checklists

The *Guidelines* produced in 1971 were reproduced in part by the Committee on Multiethnic Education in 1976. The COT proceeded to determine the redundancies between the two sets of *Guidelines* in an effort to: (1) develop the simplest list of guideline statements that were appropriate for large-scale assessment; and (2) develop a set of criteria that would be useful in judging published social studies tests. Table I, page 11, illustrates the interrelatedness of the *Guidelines*. By examining the guideline statements on this grid, the COT was able to identify and name eight factors that were present across both sets of *Guidelines*. (Six of the factors identified were not considered appropriate for large-scale assessment.)[4]

1. *School Milieu:* These guideline statements described how the local school should provide for staff development; support services and materials; and provide aesthetic experiences and release time for the social studies faculty.
2. *Instructional Resources:* These guidelines described the physical resources (media) available for social studies instruction and the accessibility of the community to the school.
3. *Instructional Development:* Guidelines under this heading provided direction to lesson planning; and promoted positive attitudes toward learning, learning styles, and interdisciplinary and multidisciplinary dimensions of instruction.
4. *Student Participation:* Essentially these guidelines focused upon student involvement in the instructional process and in community action.

Table 1.
Factors Present in *NCSS Guidelines* 1971 and 1976.

1976 Guidelines		1.0 (1.1-.4)	2.0 (2.0-.2)	(2.3)	(2.4)	(2.5)	(2.6)	(2.7)	3.0 (3.1)	(3.2-.3)	(3.4-.8)	4.0 (4.1-.6)	5.0 (5.1)	(5.2-.3)	(5.4-.7)	6.0 (6.1-.6)	7.0 (7.1-.2)	(7.3-.4)	8.0 (8.1-.8)	9.0 (1.1-.7)	FACTOR NAMES
1.0							X									X					Instr. Resources
	(1.1)		X	X					X	X											S/S-Content
	(1.2–.5)						X									X					Instr. Resources
2.0	(2.1–.5)																			X	School Milieu
3.0	(3.1)																			X	School Milieu
4.0	(4.1–.6)																			X	School Milieu
5.0	(5.1–.2)											X	X		X			X			Instr. Dev.
6.0	(6.1–.4)	1																			Self-Worth[1]
7.0	(7.1–.7)		X	X					X	X											S/S-Content
8.0	(8.1–.2)													X			X				S/S-Skills
9.0	(9.1–.2)		X	X					X	X											S/S-Content
10.0	(10.1–.4)		X	X					X	X											S/S-Content
11.0	(11.1–6.6)													X			X				S/S-Skills
	(11.7)	X				X		X													St. Participation
	(11.8)	1																			Self-Worth[1]
12.0	(12.1–.2)	1																			Self-Worth[1]
13.0	(13.1–.2)		X	X					X	X											S/S-Content
	(13.3–.5)						X									X					Instr. Resources
	(13.6)													X			X				S/S-Skills
14.0	(14.1–.3)		X	X					X	X											S/S-Content
15.0	(15.1–.2)		X	X					X	X											S/S-Content
16.0	(16.1–.2)													X			X				S/S-Skills
17.0	(17.1–.2)		X	X					X	X											S/S-Content
	(17.3)													X			X				S/S-Skills
18.0	(18.1–.2)		X	X					X	X											S/S-Content
19.0	(19.1–.2)																			X	School Milieu
	(19.3–.6)		X	X					X	X											S/S-Content
20.0	(20.1–.4)		X	X					X	X											S/S-Content
21.0	(21.1–.3)						X									X					Instr. Resources
22.0	(22.1–.2)																		X		Evaluation
23.0	(23.1–.5)																		X		Evaluation
FACTOR NAMES		St. Part.	S/S-Content	S/S-Skills	S/S-Content	St. Part.	Instr. Res.	St. Part.	S/S-Content	S/S-Skills	S/S-Content	Instr. Dev.	Instr. Dev.	S/S-Skills	Instr. Dev.	Insr. Res.	S/S-Skills	Instr. Dev.	Evaluation	School Milieu	

[1]Note: Self-worth relates closely with student participation under 1.0 *NCSS Guidelines* (1971).

5. *Self-worth:*[5] These guidelines attended to the development of self, individual dignity, and the dignity of others.
6. *Evaluation:*[6] Guidelines under this category provided directions for the development of local and large-scale assessment of social studies instruction.

The remaining two factors identified were named Scope and Sequence-Content (SSCon) and Scope and Sequence-Skills (SSSkill); both were rated as appropriate for large-scale assessment and subsequently as descriptive criteria for judging social studies tests.

The COT examined the SSCon factor first—anticipating that these statements from the *Guidelines* would best describe how the original NCSS committees had defined "social studies education." A series of questions was directed toward this factor.[7]

- *What is the conceptual nature of social studies education?*
- *What are the content (discipline) areas to be included in the social studies curriculum?*
- *What issues (topics), if any, are constant in the social studies curriculum?*
- *What sequencing of content, if any, should be considered within the social studies curriculum?*

The statements grouped under this factor were discussed individually as the COT sought to produce a set of criteria that would have utility in the analysis of social studies tests. The SSCon criteria were summarized as follows:

1. The social studies curriculum should draw content from history and the social sciences with some representation from related subject fields such as law, psychology, etc.
2. The social studies curriculum should include enduring issues (problems), as reflected in contemporary society.
3. Within the framework of the traditional disciplines and social issues, the social studies curriculum must include holistic views of ethnic groups—concepts, facts, and values. Tokenism should be eliminated.

While the committee found that most of the guideline statements contributed positively to the development of the above criteria, there were some statements that lacked any utility. For example, *Guideline* 3.8 (1971) states "Does the program include a careful selection of that knowledge of most worth?" The committee could not determine "worth."

The SSSkill factor was considered next, with the following questions directed toward these guidelines:

- *What operational differences exist between the skill descriptors for thought processes—e.g., inquiry, decision-making, critical thinking?*
- *What skills, if any, are basic to or essentially the domain of social studies education?*
- *Is there a hierarchy, or hierarchies, of social studies skills?*

Following extended discussions of the individual guideline statements, the following SSSkill criteria were established:[8]

1. The social studies curriculum should provide for the development of procedural (access) skills—e.g., using references, maps, graphs, visuals, tables, and timelines.
2. The social studies curriculum should provide for the development of information processing skills—specifically, inferencing, comparing and contrasting, classifying, hypothesizing, generalizing, and interpreting.
3. The social studies curriculum should provide for a hierarchy of skill development—simple to complex.
4. Ethnic content and concepts should be used frequently as the substance for the practice and development of social studies skills.

The summary criteria from the SSCon and the SSSkill factors became the basis for the development of a standard form for the review and analysis of social studies tests. Following each of several pilots, the COT revised the review form to promote the clearest definitions of social studies terms and categories. The Test Review Instrument appears on pages 14 and 15.

Selecting a useful sample of social studies tests for analysis was difficult. Special subject tests were excluded from the sample, partly because of constraints on committee time, but mostly because an item analysis of these tests would provide a distorted picture of the SSCon guidelines. Secondly, the COT excluded non-content specific psychological tests from the sample on the basis that these tests are too numerous and too diverse in their assessment qualities and are generally more suited for assessment of local curriculum goals. Finally, the committee chose to examine only those sections of each test designated "social studies." Frequently, the skills and sometimes the content of social studies described in the *Guidelines* could be found under language arts, reading, mathematics, and/or science sections of the achievement tests. However, since scores on achievement tests are not reported for specific skill functions or content dimensions, it was judged that analyses of the other than social studies sections of the tests would produce little knowledge of value. The COT did include in the analyses those tests that had been uniquely adapted for individual states and those tests that were produced especially to assess statewide objectives. The test sample included seventeen commercial achievement tests and ten state tests.[9]

While the COT rated each test item against the criteria derived from the *Guidelines*, no committee member felt that the quantitative data produced on the Test Review Instrument represented the information with precision. The committee had no quantitative standards to apply; for example, the percentage of a test that should involve ethnic items or pervasive issues.[10]

TEST REVIEW INSTRUMENT

Test Name _____   Publisher _____

Form/Level_____   Total Items _____

I. Scope and Sequence Content

A. Item Content (Stimulus)

Breadth Across Disciplines

Item Numbers   *Total*

Economics _____ _____
  (use of resources)
  (consumerism)
Geography _____ _____
American History _____ _____
World History_____ _____
Soc./Anth. _____ _____
Government _____ _____
Affect _____ _____
Law_____ _____
Other_____ _____
  (careers)

Pervasive Social Issues

Item Numbers   *Total*

War_____ _____
Human Rights_____ _____
  (discrimination)
  (religious conflict)
  (racism)
Conservation _____ _____
  (pollution)
  (population)
Urbanism_____ _____
Soc. Welfare_____ _____
Income Dist._____ _____
                Total (PSI) _____
Ratio with
  Total = ____%

Ethnic Content

                          Total
Ethnic Questions_____ _____

  Ethnic Symbols/Heroes (No.)
    (tokenism)   _____

  Ethnic Concepts   (No.) _____

Ratio with
  Total = ____%

Source of Ethnicity

                          Total
Black_____ _____
Latino _____ _____
Asian_____ _____
Native American _____ _____
Jewish _____ _____
European_____ _____
Other_____ _____

B. Response Processes

Simple Recall _____

_____   Number _____ %   Total _____

Other_____   Number _____ %   Total _____

II. Scope and Sequence-Skills

A. Distribution of Pictorial/Reference Skills

	Item Numbers	*Total*
Tables	_____	_____
Location (Maps, Globes, Models)	_____	_____
Graphs (Symbols)	_____	_____
Visuals (Pictures, Cartoons)	_____	_____
Reference Materials (shelf reference)	_____	_____
Chronology (Timelines, Sequences)	_____	_____

Total

B. Information-Processing Skills

Inferencing behavior	_____	_____
Distinguishing fact/opinion	_____	_____
Determining relevant/irrelevant information	_____	_____
Classifying	_____	_____
Comparing/contrasting	_____	_____
Hypothesis generation/prediction	_____	_____
Hypothesis testing	_____	_____
Forming generalizations	_____	_____
Evaluating sources of information	_____	_____
Interpreting	_____	_____
Identifying problem	_____	_____
Other	_____	_____

C. Evaluation

Judges worth of decisions/values   _____   _____

FINDINGS

In the process of deriving the social studies content factor from the *Guidelines*, it became clear that the *Guidelines* contained broad criteria identifying content areas for inclusion in the social studies curriculum. Specifically, the *Guidelines* require that social studies programs include traditional disciplines (geography, government, and history); "related" and supportive subjects (law, psychology); and pervasive social issues as well as topics of ethnic concern. It was equally clear, however, that the *Guidelines* did not provide much insight into social studies as a discipline or as a construct of sequenced concepts. In fact, the COT found that definitive characteristics of the social studies were noticeably avoided in the *Guidelines*.

Observation #1: **Commercial tests of social studies generally sample the traditional and extant social studies curriculum offerings quite well. Special purpose state tests were more likely to include "related" social studies content not found on national tests.**

In support of this observation, the COT found that the items on tests generally reflected an emphasis on geography in the lower grades, while tests for the secondary grades contained many more items on American history and American government. Items with economics content were most often included on tests for the middle-school grades. World history and sociology were fairly well represented on the secondary-school level tests, particularly when one considers the limited curriculum space afforded those subjects.

State achievement tests in social studies generally reflected the same pattern as commercial tests, although there were varying degrees of emphasis on traditional subjects. Some of the state tests were modeled after the assessment program of the National Assessment of Educational Progress (NAEP). These tests generally included item clusters representing the "related" social studies subjects and/or special topics (citizenship, psychology, consumerism), in addition to items assessing knowledge of American government and history. In sharp contrast, state competency tests tended to cluster test items around topics of popular, contemporary concern—e.g., business economics, law, careers, and voting.

Observation #2: **Pervasive social issues were seldom the subject of test items on commercial tests and were even less often included on the various state tests.**

Aware that the *Guidelines* specifically pointed up the importance of enduring social issues (problems) in the social studies curriculum, the COT generously assigned text items to social issue categories whenever possible. In fact, social issues that were anticipated (e.g., racism, sexism, or social welfare) were so infrequently included on the tests that the COT grouped these issues under a single category labeled human rights. Even with such broad definitions of social issues, the COT was able to identify only two clusters of test items that could be considered social issues—human rights and conservation.

The COT was forced to conclude that most social issues are not sufficiently pervasive to be included in the public school curricula or that testmakers were not sufficiently sensitive to the existence of such issues. While it was understood that a test of limited length could not include a large number of social issues, it appeared that significant social issues were judiciously avoided—e.g., income distribution, social welfare, sexism.

Observation #3: While ethnic tokenism was generally avoided on state and commercial tests, holistic views of ethnic groups were not adequately represented.

The number of items that contained ethnic content was a low proportion of all items on the commercial and state tests. The COT found little tokenism—that is, the use of recall items focused upon ethnic heroes—but it was disappointed to discover that test publishers had not improved significantly in the use of ethnic content for item stimuli. Test publishers would benefit from a careful analysis of the 1976 *Multiethnic Guidelines*. Competency tests in the various states generally ignored ethnic content.

The *Guidelines* were explicitly clear about the importance of information-acquisition skills and information-processing skills, although the latter category of skills was not clearly defined. In fact, *Guideline* (1976) *13.6* distinctly requires that the social studies curriculum provide for the development of a hierarchy of social studies, but the *Guidelines* failed to provide context clues on what the hierarchy should be.

Observation #4: Commercial tests generally reflect an appropriate balance between simple recall (knowledge) type items and items requiring skill applications. Skill-type items were considerably more prevalent on commercial tests than on state tests.

Committee members independently rated each item from the test sample as requiring simple recall of information regardless of the complexity of content or as requiring a skill application type of response. The COT concluded that test publishers were generally concerned about maintaining a reasonable balance between knowledge and skill items. State tests were much more variable in this regard. Some state competency tests were totally composed of recall items, a condition true for some portions of the NAEP-type state tests. Overall the state tests appeared to be designed to test knowledge objectives rather than to test skill performances.

Observation #5: **Information-acquisition skills—using tables, maps, graphs, visuals, references and timelines—were adequately sampled and represented on commercial tests and those state tests including skill performances.**[11]

All information-acquisition skills were not present on every test examined, but every skill category was included on at least one-third of the tests. Items requiring the use of maps, graphs, and visuals were most likely to be included on the social studies tests; items requiring the use of tables, references, and timelines were given somewhat less emphasis.

Observation #6: **Information-processing skills were well represented on commercial tests and state achievement tests. State NAEP-type and competency tests generally ignored higher order skills.**

Given that the test publisher has a limited number of test items that can be devoted to social studies content and skills, commercial and state achievement tests contained adequate samplings of a broad range of information-processing skills. The COT found that interpretation, inference, comparison and contrast, and hypothesis generation skills were most frequently included on tests, while fact versus opinion, relevant versus irrelevant, classification, hypothesis testing, and problem-identification skills were more likely to be omitted. It should be noted that the COT had considerable difficulty in classifying and identifying items requiring information-processing skills. It was difficult, for example, to differentiate between items requiring inferencing behavior and those items requiring the student to generate hypotheses. The *Guidelines* included references to these skills, but the descriptions provided no definitive criteria that could be applied by the committee.[12]

Observation #7: **While test publishers provide items testing a range of skills, they do not report subscores for skill categories, nor do they define the skill categories (or sequences) used for test development.**

The *Guidelines* require that the social studies curriculum provide for student experiences in "methods of inquiry," "decision making," and "processing social data." Further, the *Guidelines* suggest that a progression of "abilities" (skills)—simple to complex—should be taught in the social studies. Unfortunately, the *Guidelines* do not contain descriptive criteria for these skill clusters. The COT was forced to conclude that the *Guidelines* had not provided test publishers with much assistance in developing tests of social studies skills. In fact, the committee judged that test publishers were ahead of the profession in demonstrating concern for social studies skills.

What remains confusing is why test publishers have paid so much attention to the more advanced information-processing skills, since they do not report student scores on item clusters representative of these skills. Perhaps, more importantly, test publishers do not define or describe the cognitive skill "roadmap" used to construct or select items for inclusion on their tests.

Observation #8: **The process of valuing in particular and the affective domain in general were noticeably absent from the commercial tests and from most state tests.**

Little evidence can be found on any of the social studies tests that would indicate that the affective area receives much consideration for large-scale assessment programs. While some test items appeared to be value-laden—e.g., "there is little governmental control in our economic system"—the tests contained very few items involving the student in the valuing process. Some sections of the state NAEP-type tests were designed to identify student attitudes toward select social phenomena.

CONCLUSIONS

The COT concluded that the *Guidelines* provided a set of broad criteria that could be employed to describe the scope of social studies content; e.g., the inclusion of traditional disciplines, "related" subjects, pervasive social issues, and ethnic pluralism. The *Guidelines* were not, however, productive in providing insights into the social studies as a discipline nor in sequencing social studies concepts. Social studies tests generally contain items that sample the traditional disciplines and, to a minimal degree, ethnic content. Test publishers appear to be unaware of or insensitive to the need to include test items with "pervasive issue" content, "related subject" content, and/or extensive usage of ethnic content in item stimuli.

The COT concluded that the *Guidelines* presented inadequate descriptions of social studies skills. Certainly, the *Guidelines* statements relating to skills were not found to be useful to test publishers or curriculum developers. In general, the committee observed that test publishers have probably exceeded *Guidelines* standards in their defining of social studies skills.

Clearly, the content of the 1971 and 1976 *Guidelines* illustrates serious concern by the NCSS leadership about evaluation in the social studies. *Guidelines* categorized under 4.0 (1971) specifically require that classroom instruction be based upon clearly formulated objectives that include social knowledge, social studies skills, and social participation. *Guidelines* grouped under 8.0 (1976) require that evaluation must be consistent with (emanate from) curriculum objectives (intended learning outcomes). Distinctly and decisively, then, the *Guidelines* support the traditional model for curriculum development presented in Chapter 1—careful definition of the social studies and curriculum goals, description of student learning outcomes, and then a consistent plan of evaluation.

The COT noted that commercial tests in the social studies were invariably norm-referenced tests—the noted exception were the competency tests prepared by the states. The committee observed that these competency tests, sometimes termed criterion-referenced tests, were composed of simple recall knowledge items, a condition clearly inconsistent with the *NCSS Guidelines*.

Trends in Social Studies Competency Testing

When the Committee on Testing completed its report on the relationship between the NCSS Curriculum Guidelines and social studies achievement tests, some members of the Committee on Testing collaborated to prepare the NCSS policy statement on graduation competency testing in the social studies.[13] Others felt that there was a need to pursue questions about relationships between the competency testing movement and the *Guidelines* that had been generated by the research but were not answered in the original study. Essentially these questions were:

- *How extensive and pervasive is the minimum competency movement in the social studies?*
- *What is the relationship between established minimum competency tests in social studies and professionally produced curriculum guidelines?*
- *To what extent do the minimum competency tests "deflect" the intent of the social studies curriculum/instruction?*

A questionnaire, based on the preceding questions, was prepared and distributed to one member of an NCSS affiliate—the Council of State Social Studies Specialists (CS4)—in each of 48 states. Completed questionnaires were received from 43 states (respondents). An analysis of the findings and conclusions of that survey follow.

A primary interest in the survey was the extent to which states had mandated or would soon mandate graduation competencies in social studies and other curriculum areas and the nature of state testing programs to assess graduation competencies. The following questions were asked:

Does your state mandate graduation competencies in curriculum areas other than social studies?	(N = 40)	Yes 19	No 21
Do you feel that social studies skill competencies are included under language arts/reading competencies?	(N = 18)	Yes 13	No 5
Do you feel that social studies skill competencies are included under mathematics competencies?	(N = 16)	Yes 6	No 10
Does your state operate a testing program to assess graduation competencies in areas other than social studies?	(N = 18)	Yes 12	No 6
Are these tests norm-referenced (NRT) or criterion-referenced (CRT)?	(N = 13)	NRT 6	CRT 7
Does your state legal code or state education authority require that students must successfully satisfy graduation competencies in social studies?	(N = 43)	Yes 13	No 30
Is your state likely to require graduation competencies in social studies in the near future?	(N = 30)	Yes 11	No 19
Where graduation competencies are required, are norm-referenced tests (NRT) or criterion-referenced tests (CRT) more likely to be used for assessment?	(N = 24)	NRT 10	CRT 14

These data suggest that the competency movement in social studies was taking shape in the states (1979) and that its impact would ultimately be pronounced in more than half of the states. As other popular literature has indicated, language arts/reading and mathematics were the first and most prominent minimum competency programs. While this may be a solace to those social studies educators who oppose the competency movement, survey results show that these competency areas already include competencies that might otherwise be assigned to the social studies program of studies. When the Committee on Testing examined achievement tests in social studies, it was noted that map and globe measurement and graph reading and interpretation items were included under the mathematics section of some tests, while skills such as locating the main idea, interpreting, and drawing conclusions from historical passages were frequently found on reading/language arts tests. Thus it would appear that remedial programs in language arts/reading and mathematics will be designed to meet several goals included in the *NCSS Curriculum Guidelines*. At the same time the struggle for curriculum space for social studies may be diminished because social studies skills are less than adequately defined or emphasized by the *Guidelines*.

It should also be noted that approximately half of the respondents indicated that the competency assessment program in their state would be conducted through norm-referenced tests, with the other half using criterion-referenced tests. This divided use of testing procedures for minimum competency programs is representative of the absence of sophisticated testing knowledge within the social studies profession and suggests that children and adolescents are likely to be remediated on inappropriate or less than reliable information.

The report of the Committee on Testing raised serious questions about the sources of the social studies curriculum. How significant were the *NCSS Curriculum Guidelines* to the preparation of a social studies philosophy and/or curriculum goals? How much do the state departments of education direct and/or influence the social studies curriculum in the public schools of their state? Therefore, the following questions were included on the survey:

Does your state distribute a philosophy or rationale statement for the social studies curriculum?	(N = 43)	Yes 29	No 14
Are school districts expected to incorporate the philosophy or rationale statement into their social studies curriculum?	(N = 29)	Yes 21	No 8
Is the social studies philosophy statement based upon the *NCSS Curriculum Guidelines* and *Multiethnic Guidelines?*	(N = 29)	Yes 16	No 13

About two-thirds of the states distribute a philosophy statement (rationale) describing the social studies curriculum, and less than one-half of the states act to influence the philosophy of social studies in the local schools. Slightly more than one-half of the states distributing a rationale for the social studies curriculum indicated that the philosophy statement was congruent with the *NCSS Guidelines*—respondent remarks often suggested that congruence meant consistent with, rather than based upon, the *Guidelines*.

Social studies curriculum goals are frequently derived from subjects and/or topics that are required by state education authorities. While the requiring of a subject, such as American History, does not mandate particular cognitive outcomes or skill behaviors, traditional attitudes common to that subject do act to influence social studies goals. When asked about course/topic requirements in social studies, the respondents indicated:

Does your state require that selected courses be taught in the social studies curriculum?	(N = 43)	Yes 38	No 5
Does your state require that selected topics or units be included in the social studies curriculum?	(N = 43)	Yes 31	No 12

These responses, coupled with the previous set of responses, led us to believe that the influence of the state education authority was best characterized by mandated subjects/topics, rather than through mandated curriculum goals.

The respondents were asked to indicate what courses were required in their state and what courses they felt were most likely to contain instruction essential to satisfy the graduation competencies in social studies (Table 2), as well as those topics (units) required and most likely to be found on graduation competencies (Table 3).

The data reported in Tables 2 and 3 support the inference that so-

Table 2.
Required Social Studies Courses
and Content of Competency Programs.

Subject	(Number of States)	Competency Program Content
American History	38	19
State History	28	1
Government	23	16
Economics	10	14
Geography	8	7
World History	7	4
Citizenship	5	18
Problems of Democracy	5	5
Sociology/Anthropology	3	1

Table 3.
Required Social Studies Topics
and Content of Competency Programs.

Topic	(Number of States)	Competency Program Content
Federal Constitution	24	
State Constitution	23	
Consumerism	12	12
Free Enterprise	11	11
Anti-Communism	5	
Law Education		9
Multicultural		2

cial studies subjects and topics required by state education authorities emphasize American studies over world studies—a condition consistent with the item content found on commercial tests. Further, special topics mandated by the states appear to emphasize the individual's adjustment to American society—e.g., consumerism, free enterprise. The content source of graduation competencies reinforces the importance of American studies.

Further examination of the data in Tables 2 and 3 reveals that social studies courses and topics mandated by the states are not necessarily congruent with the content sources for the graduation competencies. While the content of graduation competencies does include some aspects of the traditional disciplines—e.g., American history and government—competency tests are more likely to contain what the *Guidelines* term "related" subjects (citizenship, problems of democracy) and topics (free enterprise, consumerism). Of course, graduation competencies are generally minimum requirements, and the social studies curriculum is much more comprehensive than a set of minimum competencies. Nevertheless, the sources of the social studies curriculum and the sources of the social studies competencies appear to be significantly different. Analysis of commercial and state tests reported earlier reflect this same divergence; commercial tests closely reflect the content of traditional disciplines while state tests closely reflect the content of "related" courses and topics.

States with minimum competency programs will conduct assessment procedures aimed at identifying areas of student deficiencies (diagnosis) and will likely reallocate instructional resources to remediate those deficiencies. If the intended learning outcomes of the minimum competency programs are incongruent with traditional curriculum goals expressed through courses mandated by the states, professionally-held concepts of the social studies expressed in the *Guidelines* will be "deflected" by the more popular, contemporary views of social studies expressed in the minimum competencies. The result is curriculum "deflected" by assessment procedures, rather than the identification of curriculum goals that shape assessment. The condition clearly aborts the purpose of the *NCSS Guidelines*.

Social studies professionals have tended to view the graduation competency movement with excessive simplicity. Rather than acting to describe and define social studies goals and learning outcomes, the profession has tended to blame test developers for their inadequacy in providing appropriate instrumentation. Social studies educators have not given an appropriate emphasis to the processes of assessment. For example, extensive confusion exists within the profession about the utility of and the appropriate use of norm-referenced and criterion-referenced tests. The COT examined prototypes of state tests that exhibited considerable naiveté about testing. Social studies professionals need to acquire greater skill in the translation of curriculum goals into performance criteria; the identification of learning outcomes in social studies; the development of appropriate tests and test items; and the interpretation of test results. Without this expertise, test developers will continue to define, shape, and assess a social studies that may be incongruous, inconsistent, and inappropriate to the goals that social studies professionals believe are important for American youth.

FOOTNOTES

[1]The Committee on Testing was composed of Karen F.A. Fox, Northwestern University; Paul L. Williams, then with the Virginia Department of Education; and Jerry R. Moore, University of Virginia.

[2]The word *Guidelines* throughout this chapter refers to the *NCSS Curriculum Guidelines* published in 1971 and the *NCSS Curriculum Guidelines for Multiethnic Education* published in 1976.

[3]John Napier, University of Georgia; Mary Friend Shepard, Indiana University; and Lynn Winters, Lawndale (CA) High School, served as independent raters for the Committee on Testing.

[4]The guideline statements classified under each factor are reported in full in the COT report to the NCSS Board of Directors entitled "An Analysis of the Relationship Between NCSS Curriculum Guidelines and Social Studies Achievement Tests."

[5]Self-worth measures do exist, but they do not provide acceptable standardized scores for these outcomes.

[6]Evaluation guidelines were utilized by the COT as criteria for making final judgments about tests.

[7]The guideline statements compiled on this factor were identified in the COT report previously cited.

[8]The guideline statements compiled on this factor were identified in the COT report previously cited.

[9]The ten state tests included in the study were divided into three groups: four achievement tests, two criterion-referenced tests, and four tests modeled after the National Assessment of Educational Progress materials.

[10]The base data for each criterion on the Test Review Form are reported in the COT report to the NCSS Board of Directors.

[11]State tests that were composed totally of recall items were excluded from this discussion.

[12]The COT depended heavily upon Gross and Chapin, *Teaching Social Studies Skills* and *Skill Development in Social Studies*, Thirty-third Yearbook (NCSS, 1963).

[13]Karen F.A. Fox, Paul L. Williams, and Lynn Winters collaborated to write the position statement published as "Graduation Competency Testing in the Social Studies: A Position Statement of the National Council for the Social Studies," *Social Education, 43* (May, 1979): 367–372.

3

Improving Testing in the Social Studies: Specifying Outcomes

Elaine Lindheim

Tests have been around almost as long as there have been teachers, and there are probably as many different kinds of tests as there are instructors. There are hard tests, easy tests, long tests, short tests, multiple-choice tests, essay tests, cognitive tests, affective tests, individual tests, group tests, placement tests, diagnostic tests, nationally-produced tests, and locally-devised tests. Testing need not be tyrannical, as some would contend, but in today's era of educational accountability, testing continues to be omnipresent.

Tests can be categorized in various ways. One common way looks at *what* a test measures. There are tests for every subject area: reading tests, mathematics tests, writing tests, language tests, science tests, and, of course, social studies tests. Categorizing tests according to their content provides one way of sorting out the vast array of available measures.

Another way of categorizing tests looks at how the scores from a test will be interpreted. One common use of test scores allows for the ranking of examinees. Comparisons are made, showing that Bill is the best speller in the class or that Sue does better in mathematics than sixty percent of the other third graders who took the same examination she did. Such tests are *norm-referenced* tests. They yield a score that can be interpreted by reference to the scores received by a comparison or normative group of examinees.

Norm-referenced tests serve a definite purpose. They are essential

ELAINE LINDHEIM is Director of Test Development, Instructional Objectives Exchange, Culver City, California.

in those situations which require the ranking of members of a population relative to one another, so that comparative statements can be made about each individual. Limited admission situations, such as special school or class placement, offer examples of instances where norm-referenced tests are needed. Their use allows for identification of those individuals who, in relation to the other applicants, possess a greater degree of aptitude or are more in need of special services. Examinees can be ranked in a meaningful way through the use of such measures.

A student's rank does not carry many instructional implications, however, as it does not indicate exactly what a student does or does not know. Another type of test score is far more relevant for instructional purposes. This type of test score indicates how well an examinee has performed relative to a defined body of content, rather than relative to the other students who took the examination. In this instance, Bill's spelling score or Sue's mathematics score indicates how much of a specified domain of knowledge he or she has mastered, rather than how many fellow students either one can outperform. The type of test that allows for such score interpretations is a *criterion-referenced* test. Criterion-referenced tests are specially constructed so that they will yield scores that describe an examinee's status with respect to a well defined behavioral domain.

You cannot usually tell whether a test is criterion-referenced or norm-referenced merely by examining its test items. A question about American history from a norm-referenced social studies achievement test, for example, would probably look very much like a question about American history from a criterion-referenced social studies test. The two tests can be told apart, however, by considering their individual blueprints or *test specifications*. Test specifications provide a description of what a test measures. In the case of a norm-referenced test, the specifications supply a very general definition of the areas of content eligible for sampling by the test items. The specifications for a social studies test may note that the test will measure American history from 1770–1850, with items pertaining to major events during that period. The specifications probably will not go much further in pinning down exactly what content from that period of history will be eligible for testing. The individuals developing the test items from those specifications usually have a great deal of latitude in determining the questions they will write. This latitude and lack of specificity about the tested skills present many problems for the teachers who must help students master those skills. Norm-referenced test specifications do not provide teachers with a clear definition of what a student must learn in order to attain the tested skills.

In comparison, the test specifications for a criterion-referenced test define with far greater precision exactly what content is eligible for testing, as well as the manner in which that content will be measured. This quality of descriptive lucidity about what is being tested is the key feature distinguishing a criterion-referenced test. The descriptive scheme accompanying a criterion-referenced test explicates the behavioral domain that is measured by the test itself. This carefully described domain then becomes the criterion against which an individual examinee's performance can be referenced and interpreted. Equally as important, the carefully described domain can be provided to teachers, so that they can plan instructional sequences targeted directly at the skills.

DIFFERENT TYPES
OF CRITERION-REFERENCED TESTS

Criterion-referenced tests can be classified according to the level of detail associated with their accompanying descriptive schemes. One type of criterion-referenced test, commonly called an *objective-referenced* test, is based on the discrete behavioral objectives commonly associated with instructional sequences. These objectives themselves, often quite narrow in their scope, form the descriptive scheme for the test. Test items are "matched" to these objectives. A year's course in social studies might generate a hundred or more such objectives, as each one would describe a small portion of that year's curriculum. The objective-referenced test that would be constructed to measure such a curriculum probably would contain one or two test items to measure each objective. Because of the limited number of test items per objective, a student's score on such an examination should be interpreted at the level of the total test only. That is, interpreting an examinee's status relative to an individual objective, based on the answers to one or two questions, would be psychometrically unsound. The probability of such results reflecting measurement error or chance guessing, rather than true ability, is too great. Summed across all objectives, or at least across major categories of objectives, however, a score on an objective-referenced test can accurately reflect a student's general strengths and weaknesses in the areas measured.

A second type of criterion-referenced test, often called a *domain-referenced* test, will be the focus of much of the rest of this chapter. This type of test is based on broader-scope objectives. It measures fewer objectives, but assesses each one with a greater number of test items, thus making it possible to provide a meaningful score report relative to each measured skill. This type of test provides many instructional advantages, as teachers are provided with a relatively limited number of well described, broad-scope targets to teach toward, rather than the many smaller targets associated with objective-referenced tests.

The descriptive scheme that accompanies a domain-referenced test is far more extensive than the list of objectives that accompanies an objective-referenced test. The planning and development of such a test take rigorous intellectual analysis of the course of study to be assessed, as well as precise verbal description of the nature of each major skill contained in that curriculum. What follows is an explanation of how that process of test specification takes place, with actual examples offered from the field of social studies.[1]

DEVELOPING TEST SPECIFICATIONS FOR CRITERION-REFERENCED TESTS

Criterion-referenced test development is a three-step process. First, the objectives or skills to be measured must be selected. Second, those skills must be described in adequate detail to allow for the generation of test items. Third, the test itself must be written, based upon the test specifications. This three-step process remains the same no matter what subject area or grade level is to be tested.

Selecting the Objectives To Measure

Depending upon the type of test being developed (for example, a course-based achievement test versus a school or statewide assessment of overall subject area competence), one or more individuals or groups should be involved in the initial discussion and selection of the objectives to be measured. The charge given to those doing the selecting of objectives asks them to isolate those skills or competencies they feel learners should possess at the end of the instructional period to be assessed. After a preliminary group of such objectives has been developed, each proposed skill should be carefully analyzed to determine whether it meets four key selection criteria. These criteria are *scope, worth, assessability,* and *instructibility*. Proposed skills that are found deficient on one or more criterion should be refined until they can be judged acceptable.

The criterion of scope refers to the size of the behavioral domain circumscribed by a skill. Skills can range in scope from very narrow to very broad. A narrow-scope skill represents a relatively small behavioral domain. Such a skill might take a week or less to accomplish instructionally. A broad-scope skill represents a larger behavioral domain. This type of skill is an end-of-instruction competency that typically subsumes several enroute, enabling skills. It might take a month or more of instruction to accomplish such a skill.

If the type of test being designed is a domain-referenced test, this latter type of broad-scope skill is required. The operation of combining small-scope objectives into broader-scope skills becomes central here. The following examples are provided in order to illustrate how the combination might take place.

Several related social studies objectives, all dealing with map reading skills, might be combined into the single larger skill of interpreting maps and their accompanying legends and symbols. A cluster of objectives related to a knowledge of how the federal government operates might be combined into the single larger skill of identifying governmental processes. Or a series of objectives all focusing on economic processes might be coalesced into the single broad-scope skill of analyzing basic economic problems.

In order to judge the scope of proposed objectives, each skill should be stated in brief, parallel, form. The three objectives discussed above, for example, would appear as follows:

Interpreting Maps and Symbols
The ability to use maps to identify and locate areas of natural, geographical, historical, and political significance.

Identifying Governmental Processes
The ability to identify the development, structures, and processes of the federal government.

Analyzing Basic Economic Problems
The ability to identify the roles of consumer, business, and government in the economic process.

After objectives satisfy the scope criterion, they should be examined relative to the criterion of worth. This criterion asks those involved with selecting the objectives for a course or a curriculum to consider whether the skill described is an important one that should be promoted through instruction. Sometimes, in suggesting desired objectives, selection committees will want to include more skills than can reasonably be developed in the amount of instructional time available. At this point the criterion of worth should be applied and the suggested objectives placed in an order of priority, with the most highly rated objectives then being selected.

The third selection criterion, assessability, requires that any objective selected for testing indeed be amenable to measurement. That is, it must be possible to devise a practical and reliable means for testing the skill. Various constraints may influence the decision as to whether an objective can be assessed. For example, an objective dealing with a student's ability to produce a research paper might be assessable on an individual basis with a performance-type test. Such an objective might not be measurable, however, in the context of a statewide assessment program requiring test situations that can be evaluated more rapidly and economically. In such instances, examinations where students select answers from among a set of alternatives, rather than producing an answer of their own, might be mandatory.

The fourth selection criterion, instructibility, relates to whether a skill represents a behavior that can be influenced by instruction. If the measurement system being created is oriented around an instructional program, then only those skills which are sensitive to instruction, as opposed to skills that are primarily a function of native intelligence or temperament, should be included.[2]

The objectives-selection phase of test development should result in a set of skills to be measured by a criterion-referenced test. These skills will also be the basis of the curriculum they will measure. Ideally, a modest number of such instructional and measurement targets will be selected for a course. As an example, an eighth-grade social studies test of minimal competencies recently designed for a state's accountability program focused on the following five objectives:[3]

Identifying Historically Significant People and Events
The ability to identify major events and persons involved in the cultural and political development of the state and the United States.

Understanding Structures of Government
The ability to identify the development, structures, and processes of government at the national, state, and local levels.

Understanding Basic Economic Problems
The ability to identify and define the roles of consumer, business, and government in the economic process.

Understanding Our Relationship with the Environment
The ability to identify and analyze the natural, geographic, social, and personal factors involved in the methods and problems of people's survival in the environment.

Interpreting Maps and Symbols
The ability to use maps to identify and locate areas of natural, geographic, historical, and political significance.

Developing Test Specifications

A separate set of test specifications must now be written for each objective. Each set of specifications will be a document of several pages defining, as precisely as possible, how the objective will be measured. One possible form used for test specifications contains five parts. Each part of the specifications follows a specific format and contains a certain type of information. These five-part specifications will be described in the paragraphs that follow. An illustrative set of test specifications is presented at the end of the discussion, to illustrate the points mentioned.

A set of test specifications begins with a *General Description*. This part offers an overview, or summary statement, for what follows. The type of test situation to be used is described, as well as the key dimensions that will characterize a correct response to that test situation. The General Description is not precise enough to allow for the creation of specific test items. Its main purpose is to communicate with reviewers of the test specifications, allowing them to get a general impression of the skill being assessed and the means by which it will be tested.

A *Sample Item* comes next. This test item exemplifies the type of item that will be created from the test specifications. The Sample Item is identical to all of the other test items that will be written later. Answer choice analyses accompany the Sample Item. These analyses are derived from the section of the specifications that establishes criteria for distinguishing correct and incorrect answer options.

The next two parts of the test specifications, the *Description of Test Questions* and *Description of Answer Choices,* provide the actual rules for creating test items. These are the constraints that test writers must follow in writing items to test the skill. These rules in effect operationalize the objective, by indicating exactly what can (and what cannot) be included in the items measuring that objective. Also included in these sections are the rules for controlling the reading level of the test items. Such reading level controls are necessary to ensure that the objective being measured is indeed a social studies skill, rather than a test of reading skill. Generally, the reading level of social studies test items should be held at or below the grade level of the examinees being tested, unless, of course, the objective being measured deals with the comprehension of social studies reading materials at a predetermined level of difficulty.

The last part of a set of test specifications is a *Content Supplement.* This part is optional. It is used whenever there is specific testable content which needs to be enumerated for item writers as well as for teachers. Such content is not included in the previous parts of the specifications, as those parts are reserved for general item generation rules only.

The illustrative set of test specifications which follows was prepared for an eighth-grade minimum competency test.

ILLUSTRATIVE TEST SPECIFICATIONS SOCIAL STUDIES: GRADE EIGHT

UNDERSTANDING OUR RELATIONSHIP WITH THE ENVIRONMENT

General Description

The student will read a description of a natural event or a change in a human activity that has an impact on the natural or human environment. The student will then select from four environmental effects the one effect which is most likely to result from the given event or activity.

Sample Item

Directions: Read the descriptions in the boxes below. Choose the most likely result of the event or activity described. Mark the letter of the correct answer on your answer sheet.

> *Mountain Fork is a small town on the banks of Silver Creek. The citizens of Mountain Fork have decided to outlaw driving on Sundays in their town. Only emergency vehicles will be allowed to operate.*

Which one of the following will most likely happen because of this change in activities?

A. There will be more smoke and haze in Mountain Fork on Sundays. (opposite effect)
B. Less gasoline and oil will be used in Mountain Fork. (correct)
C. Fewer wild animals will live near Mountain Fork. (unrelated occurrence)
D. The water in Silver Creek will become dirtier. (unrelated occurrence)

Description of Test Questions

1. A question will consist of a description of a natural event or a change in a human activity that has an impact on the natural or human environment. The description will contain a maximum of 75 words and will be written at the sixth-grade reading level or below as judged by the Fry Readability Formula. The selection will be boxed and will be followed by the question, "Which one of the following will most likely happen because of this event/change in activity?"

2. The description of an event or change in activity will be hypothetical and will contain the following:

   a. A description of a specific instance of an event or a change in activity of one of the general types listed in the Content Supplement. The description will include details that make it more specific, realistic, and interesting. No purposes for a change in human activities will be given.

   b. A reference to, or a description of, the local environment in which the event or change in activity is taking place. Such a description may include details about the present state of the environment, including habits of human or animal inhabitants, growth patterns of plants, flow of water, etc. Names of animal and plant species may be either real or fictitious. Any technical information needed to arrive at the effect that is to be used as the correct answer (e.g., the breeding habits of a given animal species) will be provided. Details about aspects of the environment not likely to be significantly affected by the event or change may also be included to provide sources for incorrect answers.

Description of Answer Choices

1. Each question will be followed by a set of four answer choices. Each answer choice will be a one-sentence description of a change in the natural and/or human environment.

2. An answer choice will relate to one of the following aspects of the environment and human beings' relationship with it:

   a. use of resources
   b. pollution

    c. biological processes and cycles
    d. geological processes
    e. meteorological processes
    f. aesthetics

3. Answer choices will deal with common and obvious changes in the environment. They will not depend on technical scientific knowledge (e.g., the breeding habits of a specific animal species or the chemical components of auto exhaust) unless such information is provided in the description of the event or change in activity. They will relate only to elements of the environment that are found virtually everywhere (e.g., air, noise, etc.) or to elements of the environment that were mentioned in the description (e.g., presence of a river, a specific type of tree, etc.). Only effects on the local environment will be used.

4. Each answer choice in a given set will deal with a different part of the environment.

5. Incorrect answer choices will be descriptions of environmental occurrences of either of the following types:

    a. An occurrence opposite to an expected effect of the event or change.

    b. An occurrence which has no clear connection to the event or change.
    (Note: Since all aspects of the environment are related to one another in complex ways, virtually any event or change can be shown to have an effect on virtually any aspect of the environment. Therefore, in such an answer choice, care will be taken to make sure that the answer choice represents an occurrence that is many steps removed from the event or change given.)

    Both types of answer choices will be represented in any given answer set.

6. The correct answer will be a description of an environmental occurrence that would likely be a result of the given natural event or change in human activity.

CONTENT SUPPLEMENT
NATURAL EVENTS AND HUMAN ACTIVITIES
ELIGIBLE FOR TESTING

Natural Events

fire
flood
earthquake
violent storm (e.g., hurricane, tornado, blizzard)
change in precipitation pattern (drought, too much precipitation)
change in temperature pattern (undue heat or cold)

Human Activities

(A test question may deal with any change in magnitude or method of conducting any major aspect of one of these activities.)

use/production of fossil fuels
use/production of hydroelectric energy
use/production of nuclear energy
use/production of mineral resources
use/production of wood and paper products
clearing/reclamation of land for construction
protection of land or wildlife from development
recreational use of land or wildlife
use of pesticides
disposal of waste materials

Writing the Test Items

After the test specifications for a skill have been completed, test items congruent with those specifications are written. A set of test specifications can generate an item pool as large as the domain of content that it describes. The usual practice is to decide how that content domain will be sampled before any items are written. Either a random or a representative sampling plan can be adopted. First, all of the variables of concern need to be identified. There are a number of significant content elements that can differ among items. In the illustrative set of test specifications above, one such element would be the type of natural or human event selected for testing. Another content element associated with the illustrative test specifications would be the specific environmental occurrence selected to be the correct answer for an item.

After the item variables are identified, a matrix is created. This matrix shows all the possible items that can be written from the set of test specifications under consideration. Now the decision is made as to whether to sample items from that matrix in a random or a representative manner. Theoretically, a random sample of items should provide the best measure of examinees' mastery of the domain. Often, however, for reasons of the test's face validity (i.e., the test should give the appearance of measuring the content domain in as complete a manner as possible), a representative sampling scheme is adopted. Whichever form of item sampling is selected, more test items than will eventually be used in the final form or forms of the examination are written, in preparation for a field test of those items. The Appendix explains the psychometric procedures employed in evaluating test items after they have been tried out on a field-test basis.

INTERPRETING THE SCORES FROM A DOMAIN-REFERENCED TEST

Several types of score interpretation are possible with a domain-referenced test such as the one described above, depending both upon the purposes of the score report and the amount of information about the skill provided by the test specifications accompanying the test.

The most common use of the broad-scope criterion-referenced type of test described in this chapter is in competency certification programs. Examples of such testing situations are high school proficiency examinations and end-of-year achievement tests. The purposes of such assessment programs usually are to certify whether examinees have mastered certain skills. The type of score report that results often indicates the level of proficiency that has been established as the mastery level for the test and then indicates how the particular examinee performed relative to that mastery standard. In such score-reporting situations, it is an examinee's status with regard to the mastery/non-mastery classification, rather than a particular number of answers correct or incorrect, that is of most interest.

Broad-scope criterion-referenced tests provide the instructional planner with diagnostic information of a rather general nature. When teachers receive class summaries relating their students' performance on such a test, they will know which students did or did not master each skill tested. If a relatively modest number of skills have been tested, such subdivisions of the class may be instructionally useful. All of the students who need remediation on a given skill can receive that help in highly targeted instruction focused on the skill.

There is a second way in which teachers can receive diagnostic information from a domain-referenced test. Because the skills tested in such measures are comprehensive ones, it should be possible to isolate one or more enroute or precursor skills for each objective. Often, in fact, the test specifications themselves or an instructional version of those specifications may isolate these subskills. Individual diagnostic measures can be designed to test students who did not master the broadscope skill. These diagnostic measures would assess each student's mastery of the component subskills. Using the results of such diagnostic inventories, teachers could then plan an effective remedial sequence.

In summary, this chapter on specifying outcomes in social studies has looked at the distinction between norm-referenced and criterion-referenced tests and then discussed criterion-referenced measurement in some detail. The instructional and measurement benefits associated with well described skills have been emphasized. One form for specifying exactly what is measured by a test has been presented, along with criteria to use in selecting objectives for measurement. Finally, the types of score interpretations possible with a domain-reference test have been discussed.

FOOTNOTES

[1]The process of developing test specifications is described in greater detail in two sources. See W. James Popham, *Criterion-Referenced Measurement* (Englewood Cliffs, N.J.: Prentice-Hall, 1978) and W. James Popham and Elaine Lindheim, "The Practical Side of Criterion-Referenced Test Development," *Measurement in Education*, (in press).

[2]The characteristics and creation of instructionally-sensitive tests are discussed in greater depth in several sources. See Elaine Lindheim, *Creating Instructionally Sensitive Tests*, a paper presented at the annual meeting of the American Educational Research Association (Boston, Mass., 1980); W. James Popham, "Educational Measurement for the Improvement of Instruction," *Phi Delta Kappan*, April 1980, *61*, 531–534; and W. James Popham and Elaine Lindheim, *Making Minimum Competency Programs Work* (Los Angeles: Instructional Objectives Exchange, 1978).

[3]These objectives, as well as the illustrative test specifications contained in the chapter, have been created for a consortium of New Hampshire school districts by the Instructional Objectives Exchange. All materials developed for this consortium are the property of SERESC (Southeastern Regional Education Service Center, Inc., Derry, New Hampshire).

4

Improving Testing in the Social Studies: Organizing for Local Assessment

Jerry R. Moore, Paul L. Williams, and Richard L. Needham

The basic question that emerges from all of the discussion about testing is: "What does it mean for the social studies teacher?" Is the social studies teacher the accountable target of competency-based programs with state-wide criterion-referenced testing programs? Has control of the social studies curriculum passed out of the hands of the local school division? Does the classroom teacher have principal responsibilities in identifying and defining the appropriate curriculum/instruction domains that comprise the social studies program? The answers to these questions rest in the hands of the social studies teacher and the teaching profession.

As previously emphasized in this publication, competency-based education depends upon carefully defined curriculum goals, carefully described instructional outcomes that explicate the curriculum goals and ultimately circumscribe the assessment procedures. So long as social studies professionals—teachers, supervisors, and academics—refuse to address the issues within this curriculum design, criterion-referenced testing and competency-based education will be left up to other loci of educational authority—state and federal bureaucracies and/or national professional associations. Abdication of responsibility by the teachers and supervisors raises the potential for several dangers. Large-scale assessment (criterion-referenced or norm-referenced) has the limitation that these instruments cannot be overly sensitive to localized needs and special interests; thus, large-scale testing programs potentially inhibit the specification of important goals in social studies. Secondly, large-scale assessment, by its very nature, is dependent upon financial and distributive processes that limit what may be assessed and the manner in which it is assessed.

Teachers who believe in classroom and/or local system autonomy in the creation of social studies goals and instructional outcomes have a major responsibility to become familiar with assessment procedures. Not to do so means that testmakers exercise an inordinate influence in defining outcomes, particularly in competency-based programs. Elaine Lindheim in Chapter 3 has presented excellent insights into the ways that social studies teachers can become involved in the specification of learning outcomes for testing purposes at the classroom, school division, and state levels.

Further, an essential morality must be brought to competency-based instructional/testing programs, a morality for both teachers and students. This morality is simply that social studies programs must have clearly defined outcomes in order that measurement can clearly emerge from them. Not only, however, must measurement emerge in an unambiguous fashion from clear outcomes, but measurement must allow instructional personnel to diagnose accurately student learnings prior to testing and to target accurately remedial assistance once testing is completed.

The desirable condition within competency-based programs is that measurement (testing) be congruent with instruction. Indeed, each must emerge from the other. It is unfair to social studies teachers to expect them to diagnose and remediate students when they have, at best, only a distant knowledge of what is being expected of students (outcomes) and how they are being assessed.

A moral testing effort, particularly in competency-based programs, is one where:

- the outcomes possess the four criteria outlined in Chapter 3 (adequate scope, worth, assessability, and instructibility)
- the outcomes are clearly defined and described through the use of test specifications
- instructional personnel have participated substantively in the development of the outcomes and the test specifications
- the test specifications are available to supervisors and teachers for use in program/instructional planning
- the outcomes are visible in stated curriculum documents and are being taught in the various classrooms.

All of these conditions will ensure a match between measurement and instruction where teachers can target instruction to aid students.

ORGANIZING AND IMPLEMENTING SUGGESTIONS

This section will illustrate how groups of social studies professionals may organize and implement suggestions contained in the other chapters. One general goal of the social studies—developing thinking skills—serves as the basis for the discussion.

For some time a central claim for social studies education curriculum has been the development of thinking skills. While the professional literature contains extensive controversy over what is *the* appropriate thinking skill for the social studies—e.g., critical thinking, inquiry, discovery, problem-solving, reflective thinking—there is a general claim that social studies instruction does (can) produce thinking skills. Unfortunately, there is little evidence to support this claim. If process skills are so central to the goals of social studies, one must ask why social studies instruction is so product-oriented.[1] Is it because social studies professionals cannot agree on *the* set of skills that comprise thinking? Is it because communities of social studies teachers cannot define (agree on) the elements of thinking? Does the profession avoid instruction in thinking behaviors because it is too ambiguous to assess, or do instructional programs omit thinking skill objectives because tests have not assessed appropriate behaviors?

The absence of a match between claims for social studies instruction and the ability to define and consequently assess thinking skills has produced a void in the profession that state and national test-makers have proceeded to fill. Largely, these externally introduced (imposed) tests in the social studies have also fallen short in testing the claims of the profession. As indicated by the Committee on Testing report (Chapter 2), the majority of the social studies test items assess knowledge and information-processing skills. While the latter skills are a part of thinking, test specifications (where they exist) do not express a structural order of these skills that might define social studies thinking (e.g., critical thinking). In fact, the specifications for social studies tests are based upon general professional literature (Bloom) and thus test for a generalized thinking skills model that is certainly not unique to social studies.

It is highly unlikely that the social studies profession will soon generate a single or distinct definition of thinking skills in the social studies. The discussion of the *NCSS Guidelines* (Chapter 2) clearly illustrates the lack of singularity in this regard. What is clear, however, is that the local community of social studies professionals can make a difference in promoting thinking behaviors through the use of test specifications and criterion-referenced assessments. Subsequent discussion details procedures that a local school system might follow in developing a thinking skills goal for the social studies curriculum.

Assume that the inservice activity of a single school division requires that the social studies teachers and supervisory staff work together to develop and describe the social studies curriculum. During extensive discussions, the group generally agrees that reflective thinking is one of the desirable goals of the curriculum. The question that follows is most important: "How do we define reflective thinking?" Too frequently this inservice discussion has ceased at this point, and the social studies curriculum continues with ambiguous qualities. In this case, assume that the teachers discuss the characteristics of reflective thinking and reach general agreement that reflective thinking, for their purposes, is defined within two important pieces of professional literature:[2]

Maurice P. Hunt and Lawrence E. Metcalf, *Teaching High School Social Studies*

Richard E. Gross and Raymond H. Muessig (Eds.), *Problem-Centered Social Studies Instruction: Approaches to Reflective Teaching*.

Analysis of these publications and intense discussion produce the major characteristics of reflective thinking that this school division will attempt to develop through the instructional program.

For purposes of this example, assume that the teacher group has agreed that one important characteristic of reflective thinking is "clarifying and defining a problem," as indicated in *Teaching High School Social Studies*. Thus, one instructional objective centering upon problem identification might be:

Given the context of group interaction, students will be able to produce problem-identifying responses to conflicted beliefs and/or content (inconsistency and/or contradiction).

Reflective thinking appears to require an interactive setting (discussion) for assessment of the skill; therefore, that condition was written into the objective. The following test specification was developed by the teachers as they worked back and forth between changing descriptions of the reflective thinking goal, the problem-identification objective, and assessment.

TEST SPECIFICATIONS FOR PROBLEM IDENTIFICATION

General Description

While participating in a class discussion, students will respond to statements or questions attending to conflicted beliefs and/or conflicted context of content demonstrating their ability to communicate orally the problem condition(s) resulting from the conflict.

Sample Item

Directions. The teacher leads the class discussion using any one or any combination of the teaching strategies outlined in *Problem-Centered Social Studies Instruction:*[3]

- The teacher can present the students with a problem within the context of the content.
- The teacher can encourage the students to discover a problem within the context of the content.
- The teacher can convert the unexamined beliefs of students into problems.
- The teacher can point up conflicts within students' patterns of beliefs, thus creating problems.
- The teacher can point up conflicts within the course content, thus creating problems.

The teacher stimulates student responses by openly receiving oral comments and by focusing questions and comments upon conflicts between different student beliefs or information (interpersonal) and/or conflicts of belief or information by an individual student (intrapersonal.) The teacher stimuli are drawn from the types of questions that appear in Hunt and Metcalf, *Teaching High School Social Studies.*[4]

Stimulus Attributes

1. Regular classroom setting where students are familiar with typical patterns of a perplexing (doubting) discussion of social studies content—concepts, beliefs, and values. The teacher acts to promote student responses in the discussion that center upon problem conditions—the stimulus questions focus upon conflicted beliefs and/or content.
2. The discussion begins with a question about conflicted content or belief that creates doubt (perplexity) within and among students.
3. The time measure of the discussion period is 30 minutes with preliminary class routines excluded. Timing begins when the initial stimulus is given.

Response Attributes

1. The class discussions are videotaped (or audiotaped) for three successive days. Repeated tapings eliminate the halo effect of the intervening technical apparatus.
2. The videotape of the final discussion is the measure of the student performance. A pair of teacher observers (colleagues) replay the tape and count the student statements or questions that demonstrate the identification of a problem. For a student response to be counted as the ability to identify a problem, the response must display the following attributes:
   - the response illuminates an inadequacy in the belief and/or knowledge of a student.
   - the response is relevant to conflicted (inconsistent or contradictory) beliefs or content expressed by the teacher or students within the timed segment.
   - the response is judged to demonstrate that the student is involved (shows ownership) for some aspect of the problem.

Domain Supplement

Scoring and Recording. The teacher observers first practice application of the problem-identification attributes listed above. Tapes of reflective classroom discussions in previous settings serve as the source for the development of observer agreement. When the observers agree on two out of three problem-identifying student responses, they will proceed to count the number of problem-defining student responses in the 30-minute segment of reflective discussion. Counts will be charted for each individual student and for the class as a group. The score for each will be the average of the observers' counts.

(Note: the classroom teachers through pooled judgment agreed that this behavior is central to reflective thinking—therefore, they can readily serve as observers for each other. Two elements are served in this process. Curriculum inservice occurs as the social studies teachers increasingly agree on the meaning of problem-identification behavior. Secondly, the teachers acting as observers are in reality providing for their own supervision.)

The teacher observers use the list of questions from *Teaching High School Social Studies*[5] as representative of teacher stimulus to provoke problem-identification behavior. Using previous tapes or dialogues in print indicated above, the observers will practice counting stimulus behaviors of the teacher. When agreement is reached in marking two out of three stimulus conditions, the observers will proceed to count the number of stimulus conditions during the timed segment.

Timed segments of reflective discussion are repeated four times during the year and scores on each timed segment are recorded as follows:
- scores for individuals are plotted and observations are made of changes in the pattern of participation.
- scores for the class are plotted for increasing and decreasing trends.
- scores for the class are recorded in ratio to counts of teacher stimulus and plotted across repeated measures. Increases in the ratio indicate greater student participation in problem identification.

The preceding discussion has attended to several imporant considerations for the social studies teacher. First of all, since the profession has not adequately defined central claims for social studies education, clarity of local curriculum goals must be the responsibility of the social studies teachers and staff. While teachers may disagree on some definitional characteristics of a particular goal, the faculty must share common understandings if instructional objectives and practices are to be translated into just outcomes for students. Test specifications require that curriculum goals and instructional objectives be consistent and clearly defined. Furthermore, test specifications require that the conditions of assessment be clearly delineated. Quite simply, the development of test specifications in a local school system provides for an iterative process where teachers discuss, define, specify, redefine, discuss, specify (etc.) curriculum goals/instructional objectives/assessment. The negotiation in search of clarity promotes a congruency of common understandings for all parties.

Finally, the preceding test specification was intended as a demonstration of how one of the most complex goals of the social studies may be discussed, defined, and assessed by a local school district. The importance of reflective thinking will undoubtedly continue to be debated in professional literature. Local school systems that identify higher order goals for social studies, such as reflective thinking, must assume the responsibility for defining and assessing the goal. Teacher knowledge and experience communally shared through the development of test specifications brings focus to the most difficult social studies goals. School systems need to consider how they can make use of a wide range of assessment processes—pencil and paper tests, unobtrusive measures, and checklists.

SIGNIFICANCE OF SITUATIONS OF TEACHERS

Organizing instruction to meet the criteria for a moral testing/instructional program may prove to be more or less difficult depending upon the specific situation of the social studies teacher. A discussion of these situations follows. The goal of these activities is always to bring consistency between measurement and instruction.

In some areas of the country, school districts are not laboring under any form of competency-based programs. As a result, district-wide outcomes in the social studies may or may not be in existence. In those areas where there are no district-wide scope and sequence curricular documents, the most important element presented in this Bulletin is the emphasis for each teacher to define for himself or herself what it is each is really teaching. Individual teachers can and should be able to proceed through this definitional process, even informally, to bring what they want to teach and what they may actually be teaching (and testing) into clearer focus. In this instance it is not mandatory that any given teacher define, say, "critical thinking" in the same fashion as another teacher. What is important is that each teacher is clear about what "critical thinking" means and that teachers' evaluation of student progress is consistent with their intended outcomes.

Where district-wide outcomes are in evidence and there is some expectation that all students will be taught (and, it is hoped, learn) what is expected, the generation of "streamlined" test specifications, even in the absence of a formal test, will serve the purpose of clarifying outcomes for the professional personnel and for other interested client groups—e.g., school board, parents. This process would also have potential for revising scope and sequence charts, bringing to the forefront many enabling knowledge/skills necessary for the successful instruction of the most important outcomes.

The real power found in the complete application of criterion-referenced test technology is manifested in those districts where competency-based programs are mandated, particularly for promotion and/or graduation. It is under these conditions that teachers are responsible for teaching specific outcomes to students and where student acquisition of those outcomes are made public in the form of test performances. One of several conditions may be present in districts which are under local or state mandates to certify student proficiency. Tests may be in place with or without the benefit of accompanying test specifications, or tests may be under development/selection, again with or without the benefit of specifications.

A most distressing situation may exist where tests (either district or state) are in place without the benefit of test specifications. Typically, these tests may be referred to (Elaine Lindheim discusses this in Chapter 3) as objectives-referenced tests (ORTs). Teachers at the school or district level would want to examine closely the tests being used to see if a rough set of test specifications could be developed from the items on the ORT. This action would bring some minimum congruence between what they are teaching and what students may be likely to encounter on the test. Further, these preliminary specifications could form the basis for transforming the extant ORT into a criterion-referenced test.

A much more positive situation exists where criterion-referenced tests are already in place. In this instance, there are existing test specifications which have, at the very minimum, been used to describe outcomes and generate test items. Streamlined sets of the specifications used for item development could then form the basis of the instructional support system. Copies of these specifications could be located in each school, and teachers could use them to generate a within-school, test-item bank. The items could be written on 3 × 5 cards and kept in a central location, such as the department office or teacher resource room. Teachers could then select items on an objective-by-objective basis and use them as diagnostic measures prior to the operational test. Based upon student performance on these items, instruction could be targeted to areas of student weaknesses. Once the test has been given and areas of individual weaknesses identified, teachers can develop remedial instruction using other test items from the bank to monitor the success of their remedial efforts. Periodically, additional test items can be generated by teachers from the test specifications during workdays or inservice activities so that the bank is always replenished.

A professional concern frequently raised by this process is the charge that "teaching-to-the-test" is taking place. Indeed it is, but not in the pejorative sense. As long as the content domains of target-interest satisfy the criterion of adequate scope, the students are being instructed on previously defined, instructionally important outcomes, and not on actual items that will appear on the test. Immorality would result if teachers were not allowed to discern what is important to teach children in preparation for the test.

In the instance where those involved in competency-based programs are also in the process of selecting or developing assessment instruments, test specifications clearly assume primary importance. If a district or a state is to select an already developed test, then it must be one which has accompanying it comprehensive specifications of the type described in Chapter 3. Further, the psychometric qualities of the test should be consistent, at the absolute minimum, with the same or similar procedures outlined in Chapter 6. It is not necessary that all of the procedures in Chapter 6 be totally understood when evaluating a test for selection. It is sufficient to know that they have been applied in the development of the tests under consideration.

The procedures outlined and issues raised in each of the chapters in this Bulletin should be of aid to those districts wishing to develop their own tests. Chapter 3 outlines the specification of test outcomes, and Chapter 6 suggests procedures that could be used to minimize a lack of validity and reliability in the test scores. A little practice with the procedures in Chapter 6 would allow those with minimal statistical skills to apply them successfully.

FOOTNOTES

[1]James P. Shaver, O.L. Davis, Jr., and Suzanne W. Helburn, "The Status of Social Studies Education: Impressions from Three NSF Studies." *Social Education*, Vol. 43, No. 2, pp. 150–153.

[2]Maurice P. Hunt and Lawrence E. Metcalf, *Teaching High School Social Studies* (New York: Harper and Row, 1968); and Richard E. Gross and Raymond H. Muessig (Eds.), *Problem-Centered Social Studies Instruction: Approaches to Reflective Thinking*, Curriculum Series, No. 14 (Washington: National Council for the Social Studies, 1971)

[3]Gross and Muessig, *op. cit.*, p. 59.

[4]Hunt and Metcalf, *op. cit.*, p. 181.

[5]*Ibid.*

5

NAEP
Social Studies and Citizenship Exercises and Their Usefulness for Improving Instruction[1]

Ronald K. Hambleton and Robert A. Simon[2]

There cannot be many teachers today who have not heard about or had the opportunity to use criterion-referenced tests in their classrooms. Only ten years ago the situation was exactly the opposite. Criterion-referenced testing was new; there were few tests commercially available; and guidelines for test development were sketchy. In fact, there were some educators who felt that criterion-referenced testing was just another "fad" with a short life expectancy. A representative from one large test publishing company was reported to have said, "we will keep an eye on it until it dies." Today criterion-referenced tests are widely used and in applications as far ranging as objectives-based instructional programs at the classroom level, program evaluations at the district and state levels, and competency-based certification programs at the state and national levels.

Why has there been such a dramatic shift in the scope and direc-

[1]*Laboratory of Psychometric and Evaluative Research Report No. 108.* Amherst, MA: School of Education, University of Massachusetts, 1980.

[2]The authors are grateful to Jack Schmidt of National Assessment of Educational Progress for helpful comments on a draft of the paper and for providing us with a wealth of published and unpublished documents which proved to be invaluable in our work.

RONALD K. HAMBLETON is Director of the Laboratory of Psychometric and Evaluative Research, University of Massachusetts; ROBERT A. SIMON is Research Associate, Laboratory of Psychometric and Evaluative Research, University of Massachusetts.

tion of achievement testing in this country over the last ten years? It is probably because criterion-referenced tests provide at least one type of information which is greatly valued by parents, teachers, and school administrators and which cannot be obtained as well from other types of tests—criterion-referenced tests provide specific and detailed information about student levels of performance in relation to sets of well-defined objectives (or competencies). The objectives of interest might be those that define, for example, a social studies curriculum, or the requirements for promotion from one grade to the next or for high school graduation. In the early 1970s criterion-referenced testing was plagued by confusion and debate over definitions, applications, and technical matters (for example, procedures for test development and assessment of test score reliability and validity were not adequately researched and developed); by 1980, substantial progress had been made toward the establishment of a practical and usable criterion-referenced testing technology (Berk, 1980; Hambleton, 1980; Popham, 1978). The technology is now widely used in building tests and reporting and using test scores by classroom teachers, school districts, state departments of education, commercial test publishers, and test contracting agencies.

One of the most successful testing programs and one which draws on some of the available criterion-referenced testing technology is conducted by the National Assessment of Educational Progress (NAEP). In this chapter we will (1) introduce NAEP, and its goals and activities in relation to social studies and citizenship assessment; (2) review the methods NAEP uses to build tests, and (3) suggest some possible uses of NAEP resources, and methods for use in classroom instruction.

DESCRIPTION OF NAEP

NAEP was conceived in 1963 and began its first national assessment in 1969. Initial funding came from private foundations (primarily the Carnegie Corporation) but it is now totally funded by the federal government. The project has been funded with as much as $6 million (in 1972 and 1973) and as little as $3.9 million (in 1979).

The overall goal of NAEP is to "measure the knowledge, skills and attitudes possessed by young Americans at key points in the education system . . . and to measure changes (growth or decline) in their educational attainments over time" (Martin, 1979, p. 46). Martin also described seven specific goals of NAEP activities:

1. Detect the current status and report changes in the educational attainments of young Americans.
2. Report long-term trends in the educational attainments of young Americans.

3. Report assessment findings in the context of other data on educational and social conditions.
4. Make the National Assessment data base available for research on educational issues, while protecting the privacy of both state and local units.
5. Disseminate findings to the general public, to the federal government, and to other priority audiences.
6. Advance assessment technology through an ongoing program of research and operation studies.
7. Disseminate assessment methods and materials, and assist those who wish to apply them at national, state, and local levels.

It is in accomplishing its seventh goal that NAEP has the potential for making a direct impact on day-to-day instruction and assessment in the classroom.

There are ten learning areas which are assessed by NAEP:

1. Art
2. Career and Occupational Development
3. Citizenship
4. Literature
5. Mathematics
6. Music
7. Reading
8. Science
9. Social Studies
10. Writing

Citizenship was assessed in 1969–70 and again in 1975–76. Social studies was assessed in 1971–72 and again in 1975–76. They are both scheduled for a third assessment in 1981–82. Typically, a person selected for inclusion in an assessment will be administered a test (NAEP calls it a "booklet") with 25 to 30 test questions (NAEP calls them "exercises"). The shortness of the test assures that an examinee is not overburdened and that the test can easily be administered during a typical classroom period. Sampling of persons is carefully done so that generalizations to various subpopulations of interest in the country can be made. Each booklet is administered to about 2500 examinees, thereby assuring statistically stable results. At each age group of interest (there are four), between 10 and 15 booklets are constructed and included in the assessment. In this way a large sampling of content is possible and the meaningfulness and usefulness of the results are enhanced.

Results of the assessment are reported for the following categories: (1) Age—9-year-olds, 13-year-olds, 17-year-olds, young adults (ages 26–35); (2) Region—Northeast, Southeast, Central, West; (3) Sex; (4) Race—Black, White, Hispanic; (5) Size and Type of Community—High metro., Low metro., Extreme rural, Main big city, Urban fringe, Medium city, Small places; (6) Parents' Level of Education—No high school, Some high school, Graduated high school, Post high school. No comparisons are made of individual students, schools, school districts, or states. In fact, student names are not even recorded in their booklets.

After each assessment, complete results are reported and about half the test questions are released to the public. The unreleased test questions are kept to be used to measure change in a later assessment. NAEP makes a fine effort at disseminating the results. The reports on the results are in a variety of forms. Booklets from NAEP are bountiful and rather inexpensive. Frequently, NAEP puts copies of the reports in ERIC. Many of the reports are non-technical and interesting summaries of NAEP data. A wealth of technical information is also available on the tests. The technical reports are most useful for large-scale policy-type decisions. Of much greater practical value at the classroom level are the booklets containing the objectives to which the test items relate and the sets of released items. The released exercise set is inexpensive ($20–$30) and a worthwhile investment, and the objectives booklets are only a dollar or two. Sample exercises and related statistical information will be presented in a later section.

SOCIAL STUDIES/CITIZENSHIP OBJECTIVES

Over the twelve years of NAEP's history, both its specific goals and the objectives measured by the tests have evolved to reflect the informational needs of the public and curriculum reforms. Hulsart (1979) provides an excellent account of the social studies and citizenship objectives and how and why they have changed over the years.

The list of objectives and subobjectives for 1981–82 are presented below:

Objective 1—Demonstrates skills necessary to acquire information

A. Uses the senses.
B. Uses sources such as card catalogs and indexes, case studies, computers, drawings, films, globes and other models, graphs, maps, newspapers, photos, pictures, radio, recordings, reference books, slides, tapes, television.
C. Uses techniques such as personal interviews, written surveys, polls and questionnaires.

Objective 2—Demonstrates skills necessary to use information

A. Organizes information.
B. Applies information.
C. Makes decisions and solves problems.
D. Critically evaluates information.

Objective 3—Demonstrates an understanding of individual development and the skills necessary to communicate with others

A. Examines individual beliefs, values, and behaviors.

B. Demonstrates individual development.
C. Communicates in graphic and oral forms.
D. Gives attention and responds to the expression of others.
E. Interacts in groups in various capacities.
F. Has effective relations with people having different cultural perspectives.

Objective 4—Demonstrates an understanding of and interest in the ways human beings organize, adapt to, and change their environments

A. Understands the forces that shape individual human beings.
B. Understands the interrelatedness of human societies.
C. Understands the organization of human societies.
D. Understands relationships between individuals and groups.
E. Understands relationships among groups.
F. Understands the relationships between people and the natural environment.
G. Has an awareness of global concerns.
H. Has a commitment to human rights worldwide.

Objective 5—Demonstrates an understanding of and interest in the development of the United States

A. Understands the principles and purposes of the United States.
B. Understands the organization and operation of the governments in the United States.
C. Understands political decision-making in the United States.
D. Understands the electoral processes in the United States.
E. Understands the basis and organization of the legal system in the United States.
F. Knows rights of individuals in the United States.
G. Recognizes civil and criminal justice systems in the United States.
H. Has a commitment to support justice and rights of all individuals.
I. Understands economics in the United States.
J. Understands major social changes that have occurred in American society.
K. Has a commitment to participating in community service and civic improvement.

It is in relation to the objectives and subobjectives above that national test results and test materials will probably be most useful to the classroom teacher. In most cases the results are reported on an item-by-item basis. Also, summary scores are obtained by summing over test scores from sets of similar objectives. These summary scores are often used to compare the performance of different groups (for example, groups of examinees from different parts of the country) or to compare the performance of one group from one time period to another.

DIFFERENCES BETWEEN
CRITERION-REFERENCED TESTS
AND NAEP EXERCISES

Many definitions of "criterion-referenced tests" have been proposed (Hambleton, 1980; Hambleton & Eignor, 1979; Popham, 1978). Popham (1978) offered the one which has received the most visibility and acceptance:

> A criterion-referenced test is constructed to assess the performance level of examinees in relation to a set of well-defined objectives (or competencies).

Several points about the definition should be explained: first, terms such as objectives, competencies, and skills can be used interchangeably. Second, every objective measured in the test must be *well-defined*. This means that the content or behaviors defining each objective must be clearly described. Well-defined objectives facilitate the process of writing test items and enhance the quality of test score interpretations. Quality of interpretations is improved because of the clarity of the content or behavior domains to which test scores are referenced. The breadth and complexity of each domain of content or behaviors defining an objective can vary, but, again, the domain *must* be clearly defined. The purpose of the test will influence the breadth of domains. Diagnostic tests are organized around narrowly defined objectives. Year-end assessments will normally be carried out with more broadly defined objectives. Third, when more than one objective is measured in a test, the test items are organized into distinct subtests corresponding to the objectives, and examinee performance is reported on *each* of the objectives.

Confusion has existed over the differences between two kinds of tests—*criterion-referenced tests* and *objectives-referenced tests*. Objectives-referenced tests are tests consisting of items that are matched to objectives. The primary distinction between criterion-referenced tests and objectives-referenced tests is as follows: In a criterion-referenced test the items are organized into clusters and each cluster of items serves as a representative set of items from a clearly defined content domain measuring an objective. With an objective-referenced test, *no* clear domain of content is specified, and items are *not* considered to be representative of a content domain. Differences between the two types of tests on the matter of "content domain specification" has one very important implication for the type of test score generalizations that can be made from each test. Since a criterion-referenced test consists of representative samples of items from well-defined domains of content, valid inferences about examinee performance in those domains can be made from examinee test performance. With objectives-referenced tests, domains of content are not clearly specified and so score interpretations must be in terms of the *specific* items included in the tests.

Using the definitions and distinctions above, it is clear that the tests developed and used by NAEP are *objectives-referenced*. The correct labelling of NAEP's tests is important because of the differences associated with criterion-referenced tests and objectives-referenced tests in the areas of test development and test score interpretations. The tests are built, however, using some of the available criterion-referenced testing technology.

NAEP spends considerable resources in developing objectives. The process is a long one and includes representatives from a variety of interested groups. In fact, their process for objectives identification and review is more elaborate than any others we have seen. In addition, each time an assessment is undertaken new objectives are developed. The list of objectives and subobjectives for the 1981–82 assessment was reported in the last section. Additional features of each subobjective are also provided in the NAEP booklet on objectives (NAEP, 1980). For example, in relation to objective 4, there are 8 subobjectives and 53 separate features!

Over the twelve years of the NAEP assessments the objectives in social studies and citizenship have become progressively more global. In the past, NAEP has had items written and then, after review, the accepted ones are matched to the appropriate objectives and subobjectives. This procedure has left some subobjectives either over-represented or underrepresented when the exercises are finally compiled into test booklets. Aside from the fact that the objectives change from one assessment to the next (which seems healthy for the social studies profession but makes comparisons in terms of objectives between assessments difficult), an item which is repeated can be in different objectives each time. NAEP is capable of reporting results from the assessment on an item-by-item basis. This is fine *but* we should be careful not to generalize our understanding of the results to the objective level. To generalize item results to the objective level can lead to a great deal of imprecision in that the objectives are so large and amorphous even NAEP cannot thoroughly sample each nor even assess the "representativeness" of items included in the test in relation to the objectives the items measure.

In addition, the NAEP sampling procedure is limited in some respects. (It is worth mentioning here that the sampling techniques developed by NAEP are highly sophisticated and well executed but there are limitations.) The results of the assessment are reported in terms of the categories mentioned earlier. Limitations in the sample size prevent one going "deep" into the sample. Cox (1975), writing about the 1971–72 assessment, has an illustrative example of this:

Suppose there are 25,000 9-year-olds in the sample. Only 2,500 of these youngsters would be administered a given exercise. Perhaps 660 of this group would live in the Southeast and only one-half of these, 330, would be males. In the Southeast perhaps one-third, 110, would be black and certainly fewer than one half, 55, would have parents who never attended high school. Finally, possibly less than one-fifth of these would be categorized as low metro. That would provide a sample of a dozen or so, and possibly fewer, from which to infer population facts (p. 54).

Since NAEP is well-aware of the Cox-type of criticism, it carefully limits its reporting of results. Unfortunately, few classroom teachers deal with the larger categories that NAEP reports results about and might find more specific information to be more useful.

Another shortcoming of NAEP results is that the final scores for each item or objective are not necessarily reflective of the level of performance of each group in relation to each objective. To some extent NAEP predetermines the results by using item statistics collected during a pilot administration to decide which items will be included in the assessment tests. According to Martin, "National Assessment tries to develop sets of items with a wide range of item difficulties. This is done to address the question of what young Americans of a given age know and can do—for most individuals, for typical individuals, and for the ablest individuals at that age" (1979, p. 51). We have no objection to this practice, but it is another example of how NAEP test development procedures differ from the procedures advocated by many criterion-referenced test builders. When item statistics are used in the item-selection process, item representativeness cannot be assured. This means that the items which do measure an objective and are included in a NAEP test provide biased information of group performance in relation to each objective. Interpretations of results at the item level are acceptable; interpretation of results at the objective level are potentially misleading because (1) objectives are not sufficiently well defined to ensure the representativeness of items in relation to the objectives, and, even if they were, (2) the use of item statistics in item selection will bias the final results in an unknown way. It is to NAEP's credit that it does not interpret single group performance at the objective level. An example of the problem described above may be helpful. Suppose there were three items measuring an objective and from a pilot study it was found that their difficulty levels were .30, .50, and .90. The average performance in the nation in relation to the objective might be expected to be about 57%. But, if item 3 is dropped from the final test because it is "too easy," the average performance on the objective will be in the range of 40%—a drop of 17%! Notice that when the results are interpreted at the item level, problems due to item selection do not arise. As long as items are fair and technically sound, and measure some important piece of knowledge or skill, the results will be meaningful. At the objective level, however, regardless of item quality, because of nonrepresentative samplings of items, the results will be misleading.

Criterion-referenced tests require well-defined domains of behavior from which test items can be drawn. Typically, a domain is described by a "domain specification." Popham (1978, 1980) provides instruction and numerous examples of how to construct domain specifications for use with criterion-referenced tests. In Figure 1 is an example of a domain specification to describe a common social studies objective.

Figure 1. A Sample Domain Specification.

General Description
The student will identify the state capitals of the United States.

Sample Directions and Test Item
Test Directions: Circle the letter of the name of the capital below each of the states listed below.

1. California
   a. Sacramento
   b. Los Angeles
   c. San Francisco
   d. San Diego

Content Domain
1. The stem of each item will consist of the name of a state.
2. The directions will ask the examinee to circle the name of the capital of the state named in the stem.

Characteristics of Answer Choices
1. There will be four answer choices for each item.
2. The correct answer will be randomly placed among the choices.
3. Distractors will consist of:
   a. Names of other major cities within the state (2 or 3 of the distractors)
   b. Name of a state capital in a contiguous state (0 or 1 distractors)

Figure 1 is a rather narrow domain but domain specifications need not be narrow. Popham (1978, p. 129–131) prepared a domain specification concerned with United States foreign policy which is clear in its delineation of the domain, yet impressively comprehensive and broad in its content. A domain specification such as that in Figure 1 allows us to make generalizations about what an examinee (or a group of examinees) knows and can do with a great deal of confidence and precision because not only is the domain of content in relation to each objective clear but it is possible to assess congruence of test items with the objectives they were written to measure and assess the "representativeness" of the test items as well. If NAEP were to utilize criterion-referenced testing technology to develop its tests, then we could still make comparisons between groups and measure changes over time—as we can do on an item by item basis now—but we would also be able to make valid interpretations of test results at a broader level; i.e., the objective level. On the negative side, there would need to be a substantial increase in the numbers of exercises developed and administered.

USING SOME OF NAEP'S RESOURCES IN THE CLASSROOM

There are a number of uses of the objectives, subobjectives, test items, and statistical data which are released following each assessment. Several of the uses for classroom teachers or by those with an interest in evaluating social studies and/or citizenship programs will be considered next.

1. Use NAEP items in developing tests. NAEP sells packets of released items. These items are not copyrighted and come complete with descriptive material about each item. The 1975–76 released exercise set contains 111 citizenship items and 65 social studies items. The descriptive material for each item includes the objective and subobjective, whether the item is group or individually administered, the amount of time allotted to each item, the age groups to which the item was administered, how the item was scored, and percent correct for each item by each reporting group. More particular information on percent correct for each item by the other reporting groups is provided in the "Overview" pamphlets published with each assessment results and/or in the "Technical Summary" booklet. Two sample test items along with descriptive and statistical information are included on the next pages. They highlight the types of information which NAEP provides. The items and objectives are from a 1977 NAEP publication entitled "Citizenship/Social Studies: Released Exercise Set, 1975–1976 Assessment." The statistical data are from a 1977 NAEP publication entitled "Technical Appendix to Citizenship/Social Studies Released Exercise Set." The "P-Value" is the percentage of examinees in the group of interest who answered the item correctly. The "SE" (standard error) statistic provides information about the stability of the P-Value. The value of SE decreases when the size of the sample of examinees used in estimating the P-Value of an item is increased.

Crane (1975) describes the use of NAEP items in a locally (district) developed instrument to compare student performance in an experimental American Studies program and a traditional American His-

(Continued on p. 61)

Sample Test Item No. 1.

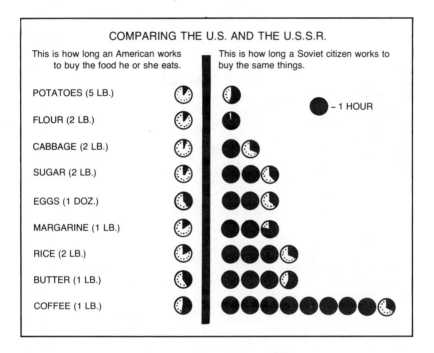

1. According to the graph above, which one of the following statements is
   TRUE?
   ○ Russians eat more cabbage than Americans.
   ○ Russians work more hours per day than Americans.
   ○ More coffee is grown in Russia than in the United States.
   ● Russians work approximately 6 times longer to buy a dozen eggs than
     Americans work.
   ○ I don't know.

Descriptive Information on Sample Test Item No. 1.

Exercise #:	R205012
Yr. 3 Rel:	RSI25
NAEP #:	205012-327-2
Objective:	II. USE ANALYTIC-SCIENTIFIC PROCEDURES EFFECTIVELY
Subobjective:	F. Detect logical errors, unstated assumptions, and unwarranted assertions; question unsupported generalizations; are aware of the complex nature of social causation and understand that the sequence or relationship does not necessarily imply causation.
Subobjective:	C. Obtain information from appropriate and various sources.
Theme:	SKILLS
Subtheme:	Interpreting information
Exercise Type:	Multiple Choice
Scoring Type:	Machine
Administration Mode:	Group
Stimulus Type:	Paced Tape
Overlap:	13
1975–1976 Package-Exercise:	10–14
1971–1972 Package-Exercise:	04–13

Timing: (in seconds)

Stimulus:	25
Response:	53
I Don't Know:	12
Exercise Total:	90

Copyright Information:
Reprinted by permission of the National Industrial Conference Board.

Statistical Information on Sample Test Item No. 1.

| | | 13-year-olds | |
Category	Subcategory	P-Value	SE
Nation	—	19.6	1.2
Race	Black	15.7	3.0
	White	20.9	1.3
Region	Southeast	19.4	3.4
	West	16.9	2.0
	Central	21.9	1.5
	Northeast	20.4	2.6
Sex	Male	21.7	1.6
	Female	17.3	1.3
Community Size	Big City	15.0	2.0
	Big City Fringes	22.6	4.2
	Medium City	18.8	3.6
	Small Places	20.4	1.7

Sample Test Item No. 2.

2. On the map below, four areas of the world are screened in gray. Each outlined area contains a small oval. Fill in the oval inside the area where Spanish is the most commonly spoken language.

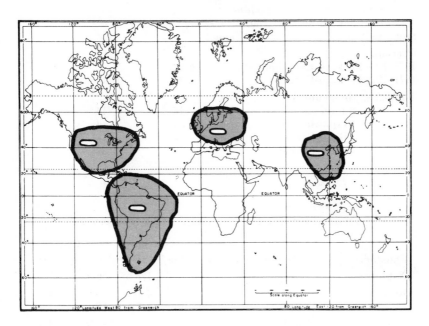

○ I don't know.

Descriptive Information on Sample Test Item No. 2.

Exercise #:	R404003
Yr. 3 Rel:	UKG13
NAEP #:	404003-327-23
Objective:	IV. HAVE KNOWLEDGE RELEVANT TO THE MAJOR IDEAS AND CONCERNS OF SOCIAL SCIENTISTS
Subobjective:	D. Understand some of the major characteristics of the geographic (spatial) distribution of man and his activities, and of man's interaction with the physical environment.
Theme:	KNOWLEDGE
Subtheme:	Geography
Theme:	SKILLS
Subtheme:	Obtaining information

Exercise Type:	Multiple Choice
Scoring Type:	Machine
Administration Mode:	Group
Stimulus Type:	Paced Tape

	13	17
Overlap:		
1975–1976 Package-Exercise:	06–11	11–12
1971–1972 Package-Exercise:	03–04	03–03

Timing:	(in seconds)		
	Stimulus:	15	14
	Response:	32	34
	I Don't Know:	12	11
	Exercise Total:	59	59

Statistical Information on Sample Test Item No. 2.

		13-year-olds		17-year-olds	
Category	*Subcategory*	*P-Value*	*SE*	*P-Value*	*SE*
Nation	—	50.4	1.7	66.9	1.5
Race	Black	39.2	4.1	38.8	4.5
	White	51.9	1.7	70.5	1.4
Region	Southeast	41.3	3.8	55.9	3.9
	West	51.0	3.8	76.2	3.1
	Central	54.9	3.0	66.3	2.9
	Northeast	53.4	2.7	67.5	1.6
Sex	Male	51.5	2.0	71.7	1.9
	Female	49.3	2.3	62.4	1.9
Community Size	Big City	51.1	3.3	66.6	4.6
	Big City Fringes	58.3	2.8	77.2	2.7
	Medium City	55.0	4.2	60.8	3.1
	Small Places	46.6	2.5	65.6	2.1

(Continued from p. 56)
tory and American Government course. The NAEP items were acceptable to the school district conducting the evaluation because NAEP was viewed as a source for independent, credible questions.

NAEP items can also be used as "anchor" items in a locally developed test. In this way, it is possible to compare the group of examinees being assessed with the locally developed test to a national sample of examinees on, say, ten NAEP items. The performance of the group of examinees on the remaining test items in the locally developed test, because of the availability of baseline data (provided by 10 NAEP test items), can be more meaningfully interpreted.

2. *Use in developing criterion-referenced tests.* Many forms of testing fall (at least loosely) under the rubric of criterion-referenced testing. A couple of the more popular types are minimum competency tests and basic skills tests. These examples are not *necessarily* criterion-referenced tests but they have, at least to some degree, taken advantage of criterion-referenced testing technology. In developing a criterion-referenced test the first step is to define the purpose clearly, the group(s) to be assessed and the groups to receive the scores, and the amount of resources available for the project (Hambleton & Simon, 1980). The next step is to specify what is going to be included in the test and then to begin writing objectives. NAEP objectives can be very helpful input for teachers who must decide on a bank of objectives to define a segment of instruction. Also, NAEP items can be reviewed to determine if they measure any of the objectives of interest. If they do, the items could be used effectively, but it should be reemphasized that care must be taken to ensure that the items selected are at least adequate to represent the objectives being tested. This may mean that additional items from other sources will need to be added.

Caution is warranted, however, in using some of the NAEP items because they often have as a distractor "I don't know." When this answer choice is deleted, as some schools (or districts) prefer to do when they use the items in promotion exams, the usefulness of the normative information provided by NAEP is reduced.

3. *Use in classroom lessons.* Hulsart (1975) suggests using NAEP exercises to focus class discussion on important social studies and citizenship skills and information. First, a teacher can evaluate student responses to a test question in relation to the national sample. Second, the questions may be provocative discussion topics. This second use is particularly good for items which measure attitudes or items which are of the "open-ended" variety. Scoring guides accompany the open-ended items in the released exercise set.

4. *Use NAEP consultant services.* As a part of its service role, NAEP provides consultant services to national, state, and local edu-

cation agencies. They primarily help design testing programs using NAEP material. They also sponsor regional and national conferences on developments at NAEP and on large-scale assessment in general. NAEP personnel are frequent contributors at professional meetings in the social studies as well as in other disciplines. Finally, NAEP provides (at reasonable cost) a plethora of information on itself, the methods it uses, and the results of its assessments.

CONCLUSIONS

In this chapter we have provided a short description of the National Assessment of Educational Progress in the areas of social studies and citizenship. Better descriptions of the Assessment, albeit longer, are provided by Fair (1975), Hulsart (1975, 1979), Martin (1979), and NAEP (1974). We have also provided information on some of the past and present criterion-referenced testing developments and discussed these developments in relation to the NAEP exercises. Finally, we have indicated four uses of NAEP resources, and material for use at the local or classroom level.

It is important to recall that NAEP, by its very definition, is national in scope. It constructs and uses objectives-referenced tests, and their results do give useful information regarding the achievements of America's youth. Thus, its methods yield information which is useful at the national level, but it does take some effort and care to utilize correctly NAEP material at the local level.

REFERENCES

Berk, R. A. (Ed.). *Criterion-referenced measurement: State of the art.* Baltimore, MD: The Johns Hopkins University Press, 1980.

Cox, B. C. An analysis of a selected set of social studies exercises: Knowledge of institutions. In J. Fair (Ed.), *National assessment and social studies education: A review of assessments in citizenship and social studies by the National Council for the Social Studies.* Washington, D.C.: U.S. Government Printing Office, 1975.

Crane, R. *The politics and process of evaluation and decision making in the schools: The Shawnee Mission, Kansas, experience.* Paper presented at the Regional Conference of the National Council for the Social Studies, Virginia Beach, April 1975. (Document available from NAEP.)

Fair, J. (Ed.). *National assessment and social studies education: A review of assessments in citizenship and social studies by the National Council for the Social Studies.* Washington, D.C.: U.S. Government Printing Office, 1975.

Hambleton, R. K. Advances in criterion-referenced testing technology. In C. R. Reynolds, & T. B. Gutkin (Eds.), *Handbook of School Psychology.* New York: Wiley, 1980.

Hambleton, R. K., & Eignor, D. R. A practitioner's guide to criterion-referenced test development, validation and test score usage. *Laboratory of*

Psychometric and Evaluative Research Report No. 70 (2nd ed.). Amherst, MA.: School of Education, University of Massachusetts, 1979.

Hambleton, R. K., & Simon, R. A. *Steps for constructing criterion-referenced tests.* Paper presented at the annual meeting of the American Educational Research Association, Boston, April 1980.

Hulsart, R. *Use of National Assessment model for classroom evaluation.* Paper presented at the Regional Conference of the National Council for the Social Studies, Virginia Beach, Virginia, April 1975. (Document available from NAEP.)

Hulsart, R. National Assessments experience with the development of citizenship/social studies objectives and exercises (draft copy). Denver, CO: National Assessment of Educational Progress, April 25, 1979.

Martin, W. H. National Assessment of Educational Progress. *New directions for testing and measurement,* 1979, *2,* 45–67.

National Assessment of Educational Progress. *General information yearbook.* Denver: NAEP, 1974.

National Assessment of Educational Progress. *Citizenship and social studies objectives.* Denver, CO: NAEP, 1980.

Popham, W. J. *Criterion-referenced measurement.* Englewood Cliffs, NJ: Prentice-Hall, Inc., 1978.

Popham, W. J. Domain specification strategies. In R. A. Berk (Ed.), *Criterion-referenced measurement: State of the art.* Baltimore: The Johns Hopkins University Press, 1980.

Summaries and technical documentation for performance changes in citizenship and social studies. Report No. 07-CS-21. Denver, CO: National Assessment of Educational Progress, 1979.

6

Improving Testing in the Social Studies: Methodological Issues

Paul L. Williams

Traditionally, and somewhat unfortunately, methodological issues in testing have been the almost exclusive domain of psychometricians. As long as large-scale testing efforts consisted of the periodic administration of a social studies achievement test, instructional/curricular personnel did not really need to pay strict attention to the psychometric qualities of the instruments. After all, if the test(s) used in any given state or local district program were published by any of the reputable commercial testing firms, the technical manuals accompanying the tests always reported—usually in glowing terms—excellent validity and reliability for the instruments. It mattered little to those receiving the results of testing whether any specific equating procedure was used, what was the type of reliability coefficients reported, or what was the method for determining the validity of the test scores.

The reasons that these issues have not been perceived as of paramount importance are many and varied. One may be that there has been little, if any, instructionally useful information emerging from the tests. The purpose for giving the achievement tests, and the purpose for which they were constructed, was not to provide individual student diagnostic information but rather to report on the general achievement level of groups of students. Even though the results of testing were usually reported for individual students as well as for groups, these results were usually reported in terms of percentile ranks or grade-equivalence scores and also sometimes in the form of a standard score.

Thus, when the results of testing were returned, it could be readily seen that Susan or Johnny was at the 43rd percentile or was at the fourth-grade, fifth month or had a score of 365 in social studies achievement. These types of test score reports had few implications beyond making general achievement comparisons among students, districts, or states. Certainly, information concerning individual student diagnosis was quite limited.

Usually, there were no sanctions invoked upon students as a result of performance on the test. Neither promotion from one grade to another nor graduation from high school was contingent upon any given level of performance on the test. About the only pressure for increasing scores on these tests came from local parent groups that may have had a vested interest in out-performing the school next door. In any case, there was, until recently, little widespread hue and cry for accountability as demonstrated by increased test scores.

Chapter 1 in this *Bulletin* has documented the inexorable shift in the purposes of testing which has marked the last decade and is now being felt in the area of social studies. Testing for the acquisition of basic skills or for the certification of graduation eligibility has now reached major proportions; and while this type of testing has not replaced the more traditional approaches to large-scale testing in the social studies, it is gaining more widespread use.

The traditional approach to large-scale achievement testing in the social studies, and in other curricular areas, has been characterized by the use of norm-referenced tests. These tests are constructed for the purpose of ascertaining the general achievement levels of groups of students and then comparing these levels to a norm group. Norm-referenced tests are constructed for this purpose; they are not constructed specifically to provide diagnostic information about individual students.

As a result of the mandates both at state and local levels to document individual student performance in basic skills or graduation competency, the purposes for testing have changed. They have changed from the more traditional purposes of testing for general achievement to certifying student "mastery" or "competency" through performance on tests more suited to such interpretations; i.e., criterion-referenced tests. For adequate treatments and definitions of the characteristics of criterion-referenced tests see Chapter 3 of this *Bulletin*, Popham (1978a), Fox, Williams, and Winters (1979), and Hambleton, et al. (1978).

There are now additional purposes for testing in the social studies beyond testing for general achievement. Concomitant with these purposes, test instruments must be developed to provide useful information about individual student performance. The methodologies used for ensuring efficacious criterion-referenced tests are somewhat different from those used for norm-referenced tests.

The primary purpose of this chapter is to describe and explain these methods within two major frameworks: the local or state development of criterion-referenced tests or the selection of criterion-referenced tests by localities or state agencies. A secondary purpose is to suggest references which provide a much more thorough treatment of the topics discussed in this chapter. It is recommended that these references be used by those interested in developing and implementing an effective criterion-referenced testing program. This chapter cannot give an exhaustive treatment of these topics. The references should provide necessary information which, due to its limited length, this chapter cannot give. *The reader should note that Tables 1 and 7 are contained in Appendix II.*

METHODOLOGICAL ISSUES

Probably the single most important reason that instructional personnel must now, more than ever before, be sensitive to methodological issues is that effective instructional intervention is expected to take place as a result of testing. If the psychometric qualities of a test are questionable, the potential for providing inadequate and off-target remedial aid to students is increased. If a test does provide this inaccurate information, immeasurable resources may be placed into remedial programs which may attempt to remediate some students who do not need it and fail to remediate some students who do.

The methodological issues which are most intimately related to providing test information of a sufficiently high quality to minimize off-target information involve validity, reliability, test equating, and standard setting. Each is discussed in the following pages.

Validity

The issue of validity is a somewhat difficult one to resolve. There are as yet no universally accepted guidelines—either as to what kind of validity criterion-referenced tests should have or how much of it is necessary—which would allow one to feel secure in professing that any given test is "valid." A general distinction can be made, however, between the validity of test *items* (content validity) and the validity of test *scores*. This distinction recognizes the fact that validity is closely tied to the uses made of the results of testing.

Content Validity. The validity of test items is usually interpreted to mean content validity. Content validity refers to the adequacy with which the items on a test actually represent the domain or universe of items associated with the objective or skill of interest. Typically, criterion-referenced tests are composed of several domains (so-called competencies, performance indicators, objectives, etc.). Associated with each domain is a set of test specifications which describe the domain of interest and provide guidelines for the generation of test items (see Chapter 3). Once test items have been written, a review process must be undertaken to ensure that the items do indeed match the test specifications; i.e., possess descriptive (content) validity. Once this congruency has been established, the items developed from the specifications are ready to be field tested.

In selecting an off-the-shelf test, one standard which must apply in the selection process is that the test publisher has actually used a systematic process for ensuring this match. In working with a contractor for the development of a locally designed CRT (criterion-referenced test), the involved persons should plan a coherent process by which a match can be assured between the test items actually developed and the specifications.

In the case in which an education agency is developing its own CRT, a number of judgmental procedures may be appropriate for ensuring that the items are a representative sample from the domain described by the test specifications.

One judgmental procedure for determining the content validity of criterion-referenced test items has been suggested by Coulson and Hambleton (1975). This procedure is based upon a rating scale originally developed by Hemphill and Westie (1950). The statistic developed to ascertain the match between test items and test specifications is called the *Index of Item-Objective Congruence*. It involves the use of content specialists' ratings of the degree to which test items are congruent with the specifications. Using this procedure, judges rate each test item as a measure of a specific group of objectives of interest. *Computation of the Index of Item-Objective Congruence is illustrated in Part A of Appendix II, which also contains Table 1.*

For other suggestions about rating scales and methods of determining content validity, see Hambleton (1977, 1980), Rovinelli and Hambleton (1977), Cronbach (1971), and Millman (1974).

Once the test items written for each domain of interest have been judged for their representativeness, empirical data obtained from field testing may be useful in identifying defective items. The generation of specifications, the writing of test items, and the evaluation of the test items for their content validity all contain subjective elements. As a result, these judgments can be, in part, confirmed or brought into question by the judicious use of item analysis data in the form of item statistics. The most frequently used item statistics are estimates of item difficulty and discrimination. As will be pointed out, in order for these statistics to be of practical use in aiding in the decision process, some variability in the item difficulty estimates is necessary.

Item difficulty indices are one item statistic which may provide suggestive evidence that an item may not be appropriate for the domain with which it associated. The traditional index of item difficulty—i.e., p-values—is illustrated in Table 2.

Table 2.
Response of Five Students to Five Items

Students	1	2	Items 3	4	5	Number Correct
A	1	1	1	1	1	5
B	1	1	1	1	0	4
C	1	1	1	0	0	3
D	1	1	0	0	0	2
E	1	0	0	0	0	1
p	1.0	.80	.60	.40	.20	

The test items in Table 2 have been dichotomously scored, a 1 indicates a correct response and an 0 indicates an incorrect response. The difficulty of each item is estimated by the proportion (p) of students answering it correctly.

Estimates of item difficulty may be used, in conjunction with judgmental approaches, to determine whether all of the items associated with the domain of interest are relatively homogeneous. Suppose twenty-five items were written according to one set of specifications, ten of which are subsequently to be selected for inclusion on an operational test form. If a field test were conducted on these twenty-five items, p-values could be determined. If any of the p-values in this item set were extreme relative to the others, it would be prudent to re-examine the judges' ratings to see if the item was identified by them as a marginal one. An investigation of items with extreme p-values may lead the test developer to find that the item was not written entirely consistent with the specifications; i.e., it did not possess what Popham (1978a) calls "derivative homogeneity" (p. 155). Additionally, it may also simply be a "bad" item structurally.

Flawed items may also be detected using a traditional item discrimination estimate or its close relative, the point-biserial correlation coefficient. Low or negative discrimination indices and/or point-biserial correlations may be suggestive of a defective item.

Care should be exercised in the interpretation of item statistics when they are applied in situations where variation in the item difficulty estimates is reduced. This may frequently occur when the intended use of the items is to monitor "basic skills" or to certify mastery learning, because most students will correctly answer most items. In this situation, extreme p-values for possibly defective items may not be in evidence. Further, estimates of discrimination will have limited interpretability because groups of relatively high- and low-scoring persons will very likely have a large proportion of correct answers, thus reducing "discrimination."

Test Score Validity. Content validity may be seen as the necessary but not sufficient condition for determining the validity of criterion-referenced tests; or, more precisely, the validity of criterion-referenced test score interpretations. The content of a test does not change from one testing occurrence to another, but the intended *uses* made of the test scores may change from situation to situation. Test score validity, then, depends upon the inferences made from the scores in light of the purposes of testing. For example, it would not be wise to use a test for the placement of students unless it has been documented that the scores from the test do indeed provide accurate placement information. As Ebel (1978) has pointed out, "If a test is used for different purposes, it is likely to have a different validity for each purpose (p. 6)."

One purpose for administering a criterion-referenced test may be to identify students who have or have not "mastered" an objective of interest. Since some standard for mastery must be set, the test user may be interested in how valid the scores are for certification of mastery. One way this could be accomplished is to have selected teachers, prior to testing, sort students into three groups; i.e., those who the teacher definitely feels are masters, those who are definitely not masters, and those about whom the teacher is uncertain. This grouping would be predicted by the teacher for each objective on the test. After testing, a raw-score distribution could be prepared (Table 3) for each objective.

Table 3.
Predicted Mastery Classification and Raw Scores
on a Ten-item Test of One Objective

Raw Score	Definitely Masters	Definitely Not Masters	Uncertain
10	15	0	0
9	12	0	0
8	10	3	2
7	5	5	1
6	5	7	3
5	3	6	5
4	2	5	0
3	0	5	0
2	0	4	0
1	0	2	0
0	0	2	0
	n = 52	n = 39	n = 11

From the summary table, a frequency polygon could be constructed to display the distribution (Figure 1). Those students placed in the uncertain category would not be displayed in the distribution.

An interpretation of the preceding data would be that 80%—i.e., 73/91—of the students were "correctly" identified by the test score as mastering or not mastering the objective at a standard of seven out of ten times. Sections B and C of Figure 1 are the "wrong" classifications; i.e., those who the teacher thought would master the objective but did not (B), and those the teacher predicted would not master the objective but who did (C). Sections A and D show the "correct" classifications. The higher the percent of correct classifications the more validity the test score may have in producing correct decisions about mastery. This approach to decision validity can be extended to other decision context, such as graduation eligibility.

It is of extreme importance that when attempts are made to collect data for determining score validity that the teachers who are making the judgments approach the task with appropriate guidance. The teachers must be made aware of the importance and seriousness of the task at hand. Misleading data may be the result when the teachers are not adequately prepared concerning the nature of the data collection and the uses to be made of the data once they have been collected. For the data to be at all meaningful, teachers must be instructed to make their judgments with extreme care and thoughtfulness. To the degree that this care is not taken, the usefulness of the study is correspondingly reduced. Indeed, lack of care in this task will make the test scores appear to be less valid than they really are.

Other approaches toward estimating test-score validity have been well described by Hambleton (1980). These include factor analytic and Guttman Scaling techniques.

Reliability

Traditional estimates of reliability are usually based upon correlational techniques. These techniques rely on test score variability—variability which does not typically characterize criterion-referenced test scores. Additionally, the basic question to be answered in criterion-referenced reliability has not so much to do with the variability of test scores but rather with the consistency with which students are classified into one of two dichotomous categories, such as master or non-master.

Criterion-Referenced Reliability. The major concern in the reliability of criterion-referenced test scores is whether or not the scores consistently classify the examinees into one of two dichotomous categories, i.e. master or non-master.

As an example, suppose a criterion-referenced test composed of 60 items (with ten items measuring each of the six "competencies") is

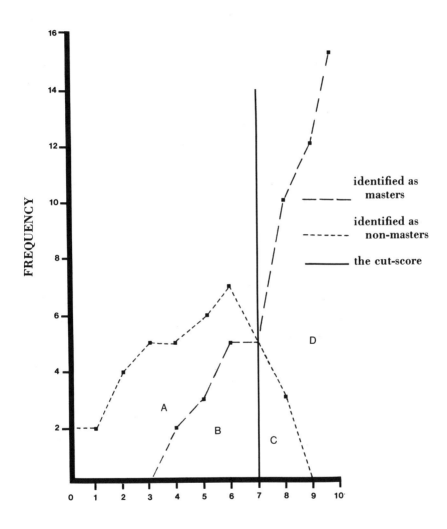

OBJECTIVE SCORE

Figure 1.
Frequency Polygon of Data in Table 3
n = 91

given on two occasions. In this case there will need to be six reliability estimates, one for each competency area. Further, suppose that the "cut" score is 80% for each competency area. What, then, is needed is a way to determine the consistency of mastery classifications between the two administrations of the test. A way that the data from such an administration of the test may be displayed for one of the six competency areas is illustrated in Table 4.

Table 4.*
Contingency Table of Mastery Classifications.

$$n = 100$$

		Second Administration		
		Master	Non-Master	Marginal
First Administration	Master	75% (62%)†	6%	81%
	Non-Master	1%	18% (5%)†	19%
	Marginal	76%	24%	

*From Swaninathan, Hambleton, and Algina (1974)
†Expected proportion of agreement

These data illustrate that 75% of the students taking the test on the two occasions obtained a score of at least 80% (mastery) for the first competency area on both testing occasions. Eighteen percent of the students obtained a score of less than 80% on both administrations. These two groups of students were consistently classified as being either "masters" on both occasions or "non-masters" on both occasions. A total of 7% of the students were inconsistently classified. Six percent were classified as equalling or exceeding the standard on the first administration and falling below the standard on the second administration, and 1% were classified as non-masters first and as masters on the second administration.

One index of the consistency of classification would be simply to sum the proportions of mastery/mastery and non-mastery/non-mastery classifications. In the case of the data in Table 4 this proportion of agreement (p_0) would be:

$$p_0 = .75 + .18$$
$$p_0 = .93$$

That is, 93% of the examinees were classified in the same way both times the test was given.

This simple proportion is a straightforward index of decision consistency. A weakness of this approach is that it does not take into consideration the amount of agreement which may occur due simply to chance.

In order to take chance agreement into account, Swaminathan, et al. (1974) suggest using Cohen's coefficient kappa (k). Using sample data to estimate kappa leads to:

$$k = (p_o - p_c)/(1 - p_c), \text{ with}$$

p_c = expected proportion of agreement, which is the sum of the products of the marginal proportions for the two consistent classification states.

To estimate kappa for the data in Table 4 the following values are necessary:

$$p_o = .93$$
$$p_c = (.76)(.81) + (.24)(.19)$$
$$p_c = .67$$
$$\text{therefore } \hat{k} = (.93 - .67)/(1 - .67)$$
$$\hat{k} = .26/.33$$
$$\hat{k} = .79$$

Coefficient kappa, then, represents the proportion of agreement beyond that which might be expected simply by chance. Thus, kappa is a more "realistic" index of agreement than is the simple proportion of agreement (p_o).

In the case of the current example, coefficient kappa would be estimated for each of the six competency areas. While in this example a situation is described in which the same CRT was administered twice in close succession, it would also be entirely appropriate to estimate kappa for two forms of a CRT which purport to measure the same content areas on an objective by objective basis.

Several considerations must be kept in mind when interpreting kappa coefficients. The maximum value of kappa is +1 and only occurs when the marginal proportions are equal. This should occur if the tests are parallel, instructional effects between test administrations are zero, and there are no practice effects. As extreme decision inconsistency occurs, the value of kappa approaches −1. The value of kappa is affected by the location of the cut-score. Different values of kappa will in general be obtained as the cut-score is changed, even with the same set of data. When reporting reliability data on CRTs, the cut-score and the simple proportion of agreement, therefore, should be reported along with estimated kappas.

In addition to the factors discussed above that may affect the magnitude of kappa, there is another factor which affects kappa and has significant implications for both test equating and accurate interpretations of student achievement; i.e., item difficulty. This factor can be demonstrated using the following information from the Virginia statewide minimum competency testing program.

The IOX Basic Skill Test (Reading, Forms A and B) was administered simultaneously to over 70,000 students in Virginia during November, 1978. The same five competencies were included on each form of the test, and the items associated with any given competency on both forms were written using the same set of item specifications. Theoretically, the items contained on either form for any given competency should be randomly parallel, as they are random samples from the domain (competency) of interest. As such, a relatively high degree of classification consistency would be expected. Table 5 reports estimated kappas for each of the five competencies.

Table 5.
Estimated Kappas
IOX Basic Skill Test-Reading
Forms A and B

$$n = 70,320$$

Competency	k	Number of Items
1	.51	10
2	.29	5
3	.22	5
4	.47	5
5	.55	5

Note: The cut-score for competency 1 is 70%, while the cut-score for the remaining competencies is 80%.

Investigating the low kappas for competencies 2 and 3 (Completing Forms/Applications and Using Reference Sources, respectively) may illustrate the role item difficulty plays in estimating kappa. Table 6, on the next page, contains the cell breakdowns of mastery classifications for the two competencies.

In the case of Competency 2, it appears that kappa was depressed as a result of 18% of the students being classified as non-masters on Form A and as masters on Form B. Since the forms were administered simultaneously, there should be little chance that intervening learning (or forgetting) was the cause of the inconsistent classification. There is the possibility, however, that the items measuring this competency were harder on Form A than the items measuring the competency on Form B.

Table 6.
Cell Proportions for
Estimating Kappa

		Competency 2	
		Form B	
		Masters	*Non-Masters*
	Masters	.74	.02
Form A	*Non-Masters*	.18	.06

		Competency 3	
		Form B	
		Masters	*Non-Masters*
	Masters	.64	.27
Form A	*Non-Masters*	.02	.07

The opposite seems to have taken place for Competency 3, where 27% of the students were classified as masters on Form A and as non-masters on Form B. Differences in the difficulty of the items may also have played a role in the inconsistency of classification. *The item difficulty estimates for the items measuring each of the competencies on each form are presented in Table 7 in Part B of Appendix II.*

Test Equating

The previous section reviewed the relationship between reliability and item difficulty as it impinged upon test score interpretation. This section expands upon the necessity for equating alternate test forms so that interpretations of student performance are not clouded by differences in the characteristics of any particular form of a test a student may encounter. It is necessary to know, for example, if higher scores on this year's test form versus last year's test form are the result of increased learning or the result of an easier test. One indicator of the difficulty of a test is the difficulty of the items of which it is composed. The most tractable estimate of an item's difficulty is its p-value. If Form A of a test consists of five test items which have p-values of .20, .40, .50, .60, and .80, the mean (average) p-value is .50. In constructing a subsequent equated form of the same test (Form B) it would be desirable that it also consist of five test items having the same p-values as Form A. Thus, the two forms of the tests would "line-up" and be of the same difficulty (see Table 8).

Table 8.
Equated Test Forms Using Items
Matched on Difficulty.

	P-Value	
Item	Form A	Form B
1	.20	.20
2	.40	.40
3	.50	.50
4	.60	.60
5	.80	.80
Average	.50	.50

Table 8 illustrates the following:

a. Form A and Form B have items exactly matched on difficulty and have the same average difficulty (.50).
b. The item difficulties on both forms are equally spread-out around the average difficulty, and
c. Having the same criterion for passing both forms (such as 80% correct) will result in the same proportion of students passing or failing the test (assuming the students taking each form are equal in achievement).

Ensuring that two test forms have the same average difficulty is an intuitively appealing way to equate them; but this approach may lead to difficulties (see Table 9).

Table 9.
Equated Test Forms
Using Average Item Difficulty Only.

	P-Value	
Item	Form A	Form B
1	.40	.01
2	.40	.01
3	.50	.50
4	.60	.99
5	.60	.99
Average	.50	.50

If test forms are not exactly matched item-for-item by difficulty, they may still be equal in *average* difficulty. Such a condition will ensure that the two forms yield the same mean test score but not necessarily the same distribution of scores.

The two test forms illustrated in Table 9 have the same *average* item difficulty (.50); however, unlike the example used in Table 8, the p-values for the two forms are not exactly matched. It is probable that, at a cut-score of 80%, a greater number of equally "competent" students would fail Form B than Form A due to the extreme difficulty of two items, 1 and 2. Indeed, a maximum of 2% of the students will attain a score of 80% on Form B. Therefore, in addition to average p-values, the dispersion of p-values must be considered in equating test forms.

A third complicating situation may arise. Two forms of the same test may have average item difficulties which are not the same and the dispersion of item difficulties may not be the same. In such cases, ensuring that the same level of achievement is demonstrated in order to pass each form becomes complex.[1]

If Form A of a test has an average item difficulty of .50 and Form B has an average item difficulty of .30, and the percent correct necessary for passing both forms remains the same, many more students of similar achievement would fail Form B than would fail Form A. They would not be failing because they were less competent than those taking Form A but because the test form they took was more difficult.

If two or more forms of a test are exactly equal in average item difficulty and dispersion of p-values, then a student will have the same opportunity to pass both forms. Similarly, if two or more forms of a test are exactly equal in difficulty and dispersion and item discrimination is the same, it would be expected that the same proportion of students would pass or fail the forms at any given cut-score.

Where two or more forms are not matched either on difficulty or dispersion (or both), different proportions of similarly "competent" students will pass or fail due *not* to their achievement but rather to the characteristics of the test.

For example, consider the case of two students who both possess the same level of achievement. Student 1 encounters Form A of a five-item test with p-values of .30, .40, .50, .60, and .70; and student 2 encounters Form B of the test with p-values of .05, .10, .15, .20, and .25. If the criterion for passing each test is correctly answering 4 of 5 items, student 2 will have much less chance of passing than student 1, even though they both possess the same level of achievement. Student 2 will fail not because of less "competency" but because Form B of the test is more difficult than Form A.

In order to obtain item difficulty estimates for the construction of alternate test forms, it is necessary to field test new items. One of the most efficient ways to do this is to include experimental items to be

---

[1]In addition to matching items on difficulty, it is also necessary to match on item discrimination, if discrimination is permitted to vary.

used on future forms on an operational form of a current test. If a test contains a total of fifty items, it is possible to add test items which would not be used in scoring but rather would be used as eligible items for the later form. In order to construct an equated form of a fifty-item test it is advisable to field test approximately 150 new items from which fifty will eventually be drawn. This could be accomplished by giving all of the students being tested in a district the fifty operational items and an additional set of thirty "experimental" items. If five forms were constructed, then all 150 experimental items would be field tested. The 150 items could then be used as a pool from which a new, equated, fifty-item test could be constructed.

The use of item-replacement as described above is not the most satisfactory method to equate test forms. It has been presented because many districts do not have the resources to attempt more sophisticated equating techniques. However, no discussion of test development or equating methods would be complete without some mention of one of the most significant recent developments in testing, Item Response Theory (IRT)—sometimes known as Item Characteristic Curve Theory or Latent Trait Theory. The proponents of IRT believe it can be used at least to ameliorate, if not solve, many of the inadequacies of traditional test theory. Two of the major advantages of IRT are the invariance of estimates of item difficulty and precise test score equating. A good, general introduction to IRT may be found in the summer 1977 issue of the *Journal of Educational Measurement*.

ESTABLISHING PERFORMANCE STANDARDS

This section will provide a brief introduction to several methods for the establishment of performance standards for criterion-referenced tests. Much has been written on this topic; and while the treatment of the topic is necessarily brief here, the citations should provide the reader with enough resource material to fill in the gaps.

For the purposes of this discussion, a performance standard will be considered to be the test score which is used to classify students into one of two mutually exclusive categories, such as non-master/master, not proficient/proficient. Within this context the purpose of the performance standard is to classify students in such a way as to guide decisions made about students consistent with the intended uses to be made of the score. If a score is to be used as the basis for deciding which students need remediation in any particular area of interest, then the score must be set so that the decision about remediation is as accurate as possible. The performance standard, or cut-score, sorts students into groups that are reflective of different levels of proficiency in the area of interest.

Methods of Setting Standards

The volume of literature relative to standard setting for CRTs has increased dramatically over the last several years. The catalyst for much of this literature was provided by an article written by Gene Glass in the fall of 1976, and subsequently published in 1978 (Glass, 1978). In this article, Glass was quite critical of standard setting methods on the grounds that they were all, however elaborate, judgmental and essentially arbitrary (in the pejorative sense). One of the most striking examples Glass gave to support his contentions was the results of a study conducted by Andrew and Hecht (1976). In this study Andrew and Hecht had the same group of judges set a standard for a test using two different methods. The passing standard established by the judges using first one method was 69%, and using another method the standard was 46%. Using these two standards, Glass estimated the proportion of an hypothesized set of examinees who would reach each standard. The derived passing rates for the two standards was 7% and 63% respectively.

Because the setting of performance standards is judgmental, does the implication follow that meaningful standards cannot be set? Many writers do not think so. What is necessary, however, is that persons faced with actually having to set standards must accurately understand why they are setting standards and avail themselves of as much information about standard-setting methods as possible.

By no means all or even most of the proposed methods for setting standards will be reviewed here. For those methods which are reviewed, step-by-step procedures for their implementation will not be given. The original sources are in most cases easy to understand and provide at least minimal implementation procedures.

1. *Traditional Method.* Experience has shown that one of the most frequently used methods for selecting a performance standard has been simply to choose a standard that "sounds good." That is, because others have established a standard of, say, 75% correct, a district or other education agency will also select the same or similar standard so as not to appear to be too deviant from what others are doing. This approach to standard setting is arbitrary in the pejorative sense and has no place in the attempt to set a meaningful standard. This type of decision is made in the absence of information about the specific content of the test, the difficulty of the items comprising the test, the characteristics of the students to whom the test will be administered, and the purpose for testing.

This approach should absolutely be avoided. A sound testing and instructional program cannot be established on the basis of an irrational approach to setting a standard.

2. *Item Review Methods.* The characterizing features of the methods presented here are that judgments are based upon the evaluation

of each item on a test by a set of judges, that no student performance data are presented to the judges, and that each judge must "picture" a minimally competent person or group of persons. It is, in part, the definition of minimal competence by each judge which can lead to the judges recommending different standards for the same objective. Therefore, the final cut-score is determined by taking the average of the judges' ratings.

A paper by Zieky and Livingston (1977) outlines two item review approaches, one approach suggested by Nedelsky and one suggested by Angoff.

The Nedelsky approach is appropriate for use with multiple-choice tests. Essentially, a minimum pass level for each item is established by eliminating the distractors which a judge feels a minimally competent person could identify as being wrong. The reciprocal of the number of remaining choices then becomes the minimal pass level for the item. The sum of these values over items for each judge becomes the judge's recommended standard for an objective. The average of the judge's recommendations can then be considered the agreed-upon performance standard for the objective. This process would be repeated for each objective. One outcome of this procedure may be that a different standard could result for each objective.

Angoff's procedure can be applied not only to multiple-choice items but to other item formats as well. In this procedure each judge estimates the proportion of minimally competent students who could answer an item correctly. These proportions are then summed for each judge over the items associated with an objective, the sum being the judge's recommended performance standard for the objective. These values are then averaged over judges to obtain the performance standard. Just as with the Nedelsky method, it is probable that the standards will be different for any given objective.

3. *Criterion-Group Methods.* Criterion-group methods can be considered to be methods which use various judgments about students along with data obtained by actually administering items to students.

The first method to be discussed is described by Zieky and Livingston (1977) and is called the contrasting groups method. Judges (most probably teachers) identify students they are sure are definitely masters and definitely non-masters (or other appropriate classification criteria). The students are then administered the items for each objective of interest and their objective scores are recorded. A frequency polygon can then be constructed of the group's scores (such as Figure 1), and the point at which the score distributions intersect then represents the starting point for establishing the standard. The point of intersection may be considered only the starting point for deciding the standard based upon the seriousness of improperly classifying a student.

Berk (1976) has proffered a system for setting a standard which is procedurally quite close to the contrasting groups method. This method uses groups of instructed and uninstructed students, rather than instructed students judged to be masters or non-masters. The scores of the two groups are plotted again as in Figure 1, and the distribution becomes the beginning point for setting the standard. Additionally, Berk suggests some simple statistical procedures for aiding in the decision process.

At this point it may be helpful to introduce the concept of errors of classification which may result regardless of where the standard may be set. There are two types of errors of classification, classifying students as "masters" who may only marginally possess the skill being tested and classifying students as "non-masters" who do adequately possess the skill being tested. The gravity of potentially making these misclassifications has significant implications for the final determination of the cut-score. If it is important not to allow marginal students to be classified as masters, then the cut-score may be set above the point where the score distributions intersect, thus minimizing the number of false-positives (group C in Figure 1). For example, the standard may be set at 80% (where only 3 marginal students would be classified as masters) or at 90% (where no marginal students would be classified as masters at a lower standard who would be classified as non-masters at a higher standard). Conversely, if it is deemed important to minimize the number of false-negatives, the standard could be lowered.

4. *Pedagogical/Political Methods.* The rather unusual label for the two methods introduced in this section attempts to focus on their distinguishing characteristic: namely, that, particularly for tests used in situations where the sanctions placed on students based upon test performance are severe (promotion, graduation), the standard setting process must take into account the political, social, and educational milieu of the decision context.

Popham (1978 b) suggests that judges use normative data collected from administering tests to uninstructed, just instructed, and previously instructed groups of students in the decision process. Additionally, he points out that data on test performance could be collected from former students who have graduated from high school, from adults, and from school board members. These and other data could be used by different educational and client groups to make recommendations of their own as to the passing score.

Probably the most astute approach to standard setting for minimum competency tests has been suggested by Jaeger (1978). Within practical limitations, Jaeger suggests involving groups of judges composed of adult persons having a stake in the selection of the passing standard. In his recommendations for the North Carolina test, three groups of judges were identified—registered voters, secondary teachers, and school administrative personnel. The judges would use an iterative process to make final judgments as to the standard, and there would be contained in the process student test data and subjective evaluations of each test item. A noteworthy characteristic of Jaeger's approach, one that sets it off from Nedelsky's and Angoff's methods, is that nowhere in the judgment process does a judge need to construct a concept of "minimum competence." Rather, judgments about items are made on the basis of whether graduation should be contingent upon correctly answering any item. To quote from Jaeger (1978):

> The procedure avoids the abstract (and probably meaningless) concept of "minimally competent high school graduate." It ensures that all judges will be fully familiar with the demands of each test item and the typical performance of North Carolina eleventh graders on each item. It allows judges to revise their decisions in light of added information, but does not subject them to direct argument from any person or group. (p. 13)

The task of setting fair, realistic, and defensible performance standards is both difficult and important. As much time, effort, and expertise must be put ino the task as resources will allow. More than one method should be used, if possible, and the consequences of the decision, once it has been made, must be understood by all.

REFERENCES

Andrew, B.J., and Hecht, J.T. A preliminary investigation of two procedures for setting examination standards. *Educational and Pyschological Measurement*, 1976, *36*, 45–50.

Berk, R.A. Determination of optimal cutting scores in criterion-referenced measurement. *Journal of Experimental Education*, 1976, *45*, 4–9.

Coulson, D.B., and Hambleton, R.K. Some validation methods for domain-referenced test items. *Laboratory of Psychometric and Evaluative Research Report No. 7*. Amherst, MA: University of Massachusetts, 1975.

Cronbach, L.J. Test validation. In R.L. Thorndike (Ed.), *Educational measurement* (2nd ed.). Washington, D.C.: American Council on Education, 1971.

Ebel, R.L. *A proposed solution to the validity problem.* A paper presented at the annual meeting of the American Educational Research Association, Toronto, Canada, 1978.

Fox, K.F.A., Williams, P.L., and Winters, L. Graduation competency testing in the social studies: A position statement of the National Council for the Social Studies. *Social Education*, 1979, *43*, 367–372.

Glass, G.V. Standards and criteria. *Journal of Educational Measurement*, 1978, *15*, 237–261.

Hambleton, R.K. Validation of criterion-referenced test score interpretations. *Laboratory of Psychometric and Evaluative Research Report No. 57*. Amherst, Mass.: University of Massachusetts, 1977.

Hambleton, R.K. Test score validity and standard setting methods. In R.A. Berk (Ed.), *Criterion-referenced measurement: State of the art.* Baltimore, MD: Johns Hopkins Press, 1980.

Hambleton, R.K., Swaminathan, H., Algina, J., and Coulson, D.B. Criterion-referenced testing and measurement: A review of technical issues and developments. *Review of Educational Research,* 1978, *48,* 1–47.

Hemphill, J., and Westie, C.M. The measurement of group dimensions. *Journal of Psychology,* 1950, *29,* 325–342. Cited in Coulson, D.B., and Hambleton, R.K. Some validation methods for domain-referenced test items. *Laboratory of Psychometric and Evaluative Research Report No. 7.* Amherst, MA: University of Massachusetts, 1975.

Jaeger, R.M. *A proposal for setting a standard on the North Carolina High School Competency Test.* Paper presented at the Spring Meeting of the North Carolina Association for Research in Education, Chapel Hill, 1978.

Linn, R.L. Issues of reliability in measurement for competency-based programs. In M.A. Bunda and J.R. Sanders (Eds.), *Practices and problems in competency-based measurement.* Washington, D.C.: National Council on Measurement in Education, 1979, 90–107.

Magnussen, D. *Test theory.* Reading, Mass.: Addison-Wesley, 1966.

Millman, J. Criterion-referenced measurement. In W.J. Popham (Ed.), *Evaluation in education; Current applications.* Berkeley, Cal.: McCutchan Publishing Co., 1974.

National Council on Measurement in Education. *Journal of Educational Measurement.* Washington, D.C.: Summer, 1977, *14,* 73–196.

Popham, W.J. *Criterion-referenced measurement.* Englewood Cliffs, N.J.: Prentice Hall, 1978. (a)

Popham, W.J. *Key standard setting considerations for minimum competency testing programs.* Paper presented at the Invitational Winter Conference on Measurement and Methodology, Center for the Study of Evaluation, University of California, Los Angeles, January 1978. (b)

Rovinelli, R.J., and Hambleton, R.K. On the use of content specialists' ratings in the assessment of criterion-referenced test item validity. *Dutch Journal of Educational Research,* 1977, *2,* 49–60.

Swaminathan, H., Hambleton, R.K., and Algina, J. Reliability of criterion-referenced tests: A decision-theoretic formulation. *Journal of Educational Measurement,* 1974, *11,* 263–268.

Wright, B.D., and Stone M.H. *Best test design.* Chicago, Ill.: MESA Press, 1979.

Zieky, M.J., and Livingston, S.A. *Manual for setting standards on the Basic Skills Assessment Tests.* Princeton, N.J.: Educational Testing Service, 1977.

APPENDIX I

A Brief Bibliography of Social Studies Tests

Richard L. Needham

The purpose of this appendix is to provide introductory information concerning a representative sample of commercially prepared, social studies tests as one means of investigating, from the perspective of test authors and publishers, what social studies is and is not. The focus of attention is on general social studies tests, and little attempt has been made to include specific tests—i.e. contemporary affairs, geography, economics, or American history. This brief, annotated bibliography does not purport to include all general social studies tests in print; its purpose is to reflect the diversity of commercially prepared social studies tests available nationally. The first part of the bibliography includes five tests which are available in separate booklet form; the second part includes tests which are available only as subtests of complete test batteries.

The information concerning each test is a composite of that provided in the *Mental Measurement Yearbooks* (MMY) and *Tests in Print* and *Social Studies Tests and Reviews*, as well as descriptive information provided directly by some test publishers. The introductory information includes title; grade range (the presence of more than one level is indicated by a divided grade range—for example, grades "4–6, 7–9, 10–12, and 13–14" reflect that there are four levels of the test, one test booklet for each level indicated); publication or copyright date (the range of dates reflects the date of the original copyright through the date of the most recent form); number of forms; administrative time; author(s); and publisher.

The descriptive comments following the introductory information are designed to indicate the general nature of each test and its sources. The comments are not intended to be evaluative in nature. The reader is referred to the *MMY* for critical evaluations and more detailed technical information. References to the *MMY* follow the descriptive comments of each test. In the cross-reference to reviews, 6:971 refers to the test number 971 in the *The Sixth Mental Measure-*

RICHARD L. NEEDHAM is a graduate assistant in the Department of Curriculum and Instruction, University of Virginia.

ment Yearbook, 7:888 to test number 888 in *The Seventh Mental Measurement Yearbook*, and 8:25 to test number 25 in *The Eighth Mental Measurement Yearbook*.[1]

General Social Studies Tests
Available in Separate Booklet Form

1. Iowa Tests of Basic Skills: Social Studies and Science Supplement. Grades 3–9; 1972; 2 forms, 35–40 minutes. E.F. Lindquist, A.N. Hieronymus and others; the Riverside Publishing Company.

A separate booklet which includes a social studies and science test supplements the regular multilevel battery of the Iowa Tests of Basic Skills. The tests' primary purpose is to measure curricular objectives that are not covered in the regular battery. The social studies test material is concerned mainly with background information of the social sciences and the generalizations and applications of social principles. Progress is measured in nine content areas, including economics, geography, politics, sociology, and anthropology, from a historical perspective and from the perspective of understanding the contemporary patterns and systems of the environment. Four skills in cognitive development are also measured: knowledge, understanding, generalizations, and evaluation. The ITBS skill classification system correlates with that of the Tests of Achievement and Proficiency (Grades 9–12) to facilitate diagnostic continuity between the tests. Unlike the ITBS, the TAP test, Form T is a subtest of a battery. Test time 40 minutes.

For further information on the entire battery, see 8:19.

2. IOX Objectives-Based Tests Collection—Social Studies: American Government. Grades 10–12; 1973–74; 5 to 10 minutes per test. Barbara S. Cummings; Instructional Objectives Exchange.

The 32 objectives-based American government tests are designed to assess the student's knowledge of basic concepts of American government in the context of eight subtopics: Our Colonial Heritage; the American Constitution; Government and the Citizen; American Politics; the Congress; the Presidency; the Federal Judiciary; and State and Local Government. Each test takes approximately 5 to 10 minutes to complete. The concepts represent those which the author considers should be mastered at the end of a one-semester high school course in American Government. The test provides the capability of allowing the teacher or division to select those tests which are applicable to their given situation.

For further information, see 8:917

---

[1]This bibliographical format was adapted from the format presented in Barbara A. Peace, "Bibliography of Social Studies Tests," *Evaluation in Social Studies*, ed. Harry D. Berg, Thirty-fifth Yearbook of the National Council for the Social Studies (Washington, D.C.: 1965), pp. 230–247.

3. Sequential Test of Educational Progress: Social Studies.
Grades 4–6, 7–9, 10–12, 13–14; 1956–1972; 2 forms; 45(55) minutes for
grades 4–9, 60(70) minutes for grades 10–14. By committees of educators and ETS staff members; Addison-Wesley Publishing Company.

The tests are designed to evaluate the students' understanding of
general social studies concepts and themes as well as critical problem-solving skills. The materials for the test questions are drawn
from the areas of political science, sociology, anthropology, economics, history, and government, and they are intended to reflect the
diversity of the social studies curricula. More specifically, the tests
are designed to evaluate the students' understanding of (a) the nature
of social organization and change, (b) the effects of geography on the
way people live, (c) the ways in which people adjust to their environment, (d) how people produce goods and satisfy their economic
needs, (e) situations involving political conflict and different types of
political participation, (f) the effects of cultural values on actions
and decisions, and (g) the attributes of a democratic society.

For further information, see 8:892.

4. Tests of Academic Progress: Forms. Social Studies. Grades
9–12; 1964–72; 1 form; 60(70) minutes; Dale P. Scannell; Houghton
Mifflin Company.

Designed to appraise student progress in the acquisition of
(a) meaningful, functional knowledge which leads to understanding
and valid generalizations, and (b) the skills necessary to acquire additional knowledge and understandings, and the ability to apply these
skills to the intelligent solution of problems. Students are required
to apply knowledge in new situations by being asked to generalize,
select examples and illustrations, make comparisons, understand
broad trends, and relate to cause and effect. Items were selected
from the following major categories: American history, geography,
world history, American government, economics, sociology, and
skills. The skills tested include: recognizing valid generalizations,
distinguishing between primary and secondary sources, recognizing
consistency, distinguishing between descriptive statements and value
judgments, and interpreting maps, graphs, and tables. Of the 120
items, approximately 27% are devoted to American government,
15% to world history, 10% to economics, 10% to geography, and 7%
to sociology.

For further information, see 8:32 and 7:901.

**5. Continuous Progress Laboratory: Language, Mathematics,
Science, and Social Studies.** Levels 1–8; 1979. Open administration; Educational Development Corporation.

The laboratory contains specific concept or skill objectives on lesson cards. Each Continuous Progress Lesson Card has a self-correct-

ing pretest that the student takes to determine whether or not he or she has already mastered the stated objective (the Challenge Test). A posttest (Performance Test) is provided to determine whether or not he or she has mastered the objective after working with one or more of the learning resources. Both the Challenge and the Performance Tests are objectives-referenced tests.

General Social Studies Tests
Available Only As Subtest of Batteries

1. Comprehensive Tests of Basic Skills, Expanded Edition. Grades 1.6–12.9, 2.5–4.9, 4.5–6.9, 6.5–8.9, 8.5–12.9; 2 forms; administrative and testing time varies at respective levels, but the entire battery requires approximately 350 minutes in four sessions. CTB/McGraw-Hill.

The Social Studies tests measure the ability to recall specific information, to read maps and other graphic material, to interpret verbal material, to select and evaluate research designs, to distinguish fact from opinion, and to employ logic in problem solving. Two major components provided the basis for classification of the skills and knowledge measured by the CTB/S & T Social Studies tests: the "process" dimension and the content dimension. The process categories are adapted from Bloom's Taxonomy of Educational Objectives and include: Recognition, Translation, Interpretation, Application, and Analysis. The content is classified under the broad headings of Physical Environment, Social Environment, Political/Economic Environment and History.

For further information concerning the entire battery, see 8:12.

2. The Iowa Tests of Educational Development. SRA Assessment Survey. Grades 9–12; 1942–74; 2 forms. E.F. Lindquist and Leonard S. Feldt; Science Research Associates Inc.

The ITED battery assesses student's ability to think critically, analyze written and illustrative materials, recognize statements of fundamental concepts, and select appropriate examples and applications of concepts. The ITED social studies subtest is designed to measure if the student has developed a basic background in the social studies; hence there appears to be an emphasis on the recall of factual information. The social studies and science background tests are optional subtests of the battery, but may not be given separately from the battery.

For further information on the complete battery, see 8:20.

3. Metropolitan Achievement Tests: Social Studies Test. Grades Kgn/–1.4, 1.5–2.4, 2.5–3.4, 3.5–4.0, 5.0–6.9, 7.0–9.5; 1931–77; 2–3 forms; administrative and testing times vary from level to level. Walter N. Durost, Harold H. Bixler, and others; Psychological Corporation.

The social studies subtests evaluate the student's recall of information, knowledge of concepts, and mastery of map, chart, and graph skills. Particular emphasis is placed on map reading.

For further information on the entire battery, see 8:22.

4. SRA Achievement Series. Grades, 4–6, 6–8, 8–9, 9–12; 1954–1978; 2 forms; (35 minutes). Robert A. Neslund, Louis P. Thorpe, and D. Welty Lefever; Science Research Associates Inc.

The social studies subtest focuses on information-processing skills. Items are preceded by stimulus materials such as a map, cartoon, or paragraph of information. The subtests were designed to test major concepts and skills, rather than specific content. General content for the respective subtests is as follows:

- Grades 4–6 (Level E): regions of the United States and elsewhere, cities, cultures, United States history, maps.
- Grades 6–8 (Level F): countries and world regions, contemporary problems.
- Grades 8–9 (Level G): United States history and government, contemporary problems.
- Grades 9–12: history, political science, economics, geography, sociology, and anthropology.

Study skills tested at all levels include recognition, recall, interpretation, and extension.

For information concerning the entire battery, see 8:1.

5. Stanford Achievement Test, 1973 Edition. Grades 1.5–2.4, 2.5–3.4, 3.5–4.4, 4.5–5.4, 5.5–6.9, 7.0–9.5; 1923–1975; 1–2 forms; administrative and testing time varies with respective levels. Richard Madden, Eric F. Gardner, and others, The Psychological Corporation.

The social studies subtest is an optional element of the battery. The emphasis of the test is on the process of learning and investigation, rather than on the recall of factual information. Respective levels of the social studies subtests evaluate the student's skills at map, globe, chart, and graph reading.

For further information, see 8:29.

6. Minnesota High School Achievement Examination: Social Studies. Grades 7, 8, 9, 10, 11, 12; 1961–present; administrative and testing times vary. Victor L. Lohman, ed.; American Guidance Service, Inc.

This series of tests is designed to evaluate the student's knowledge and skills in specific subject areas—i.e., American history, (grade 7), geography (grade 8), state and local government (grade 9). The tests are subject-specific tests to specific grade levels.

APPENDIX II

Statistics to Accompany Chapter 6

Part A:
Computation of the Index
of Item-Objective Congruence

$$I_{ik} = [(N - 1) G_k - H + G_k]/[2 (N - 1)n]$$

where:

I_{ik} is the index of congruence for item i with the test specifications representing objective k,

N the number of objectives under study,

G_k the sum of the content specialists' ratings for an item to the objective of interest, k,

H the sum of the content specialists' ratings for an item to all objectives under study,

n the number of content specialists participating in the rating process.

Hambleton (1977) points out that the value of this index ranges between ± 1, with a positive 1 indicating that the content specialists unanimously assigned an item to the proper objective (set of specifications) and to no other objective. A negative 1 indicates that the content specialists have unanimously rated an item as not matching the proper objective and matching all others.

An example may prove helpful. Content specialists could be given a set of objectives (and their associated specifications) along with all of the test items to be used in the matching procedure. They would not be informed about which item matched which objective. Each content specialist would be asked to assign a rating to each item for the degree to which it matched each of the objectives using the following rating scale.

+1 definitely feel that the item measures the objective (specifications)

0 cannot tell whether the item measures the objective

−1 definitely feel that the item does not measure the objective.

After the responses from the specialists are collected, a table similar the following could be constructed.

Table 1.
Content Specialists' Ratings of
Item/Objective Congruency

	OBJECTIVE 1 (SPECIALISTS)			OBJECTIVE 2 (SPECIALISTS)		
ITEM	1	2	3	1	2	3
1	1	1	1	−1	−1	−1
2	1	0	1	−1	0	−1
3	0	0	0	0	0	0
4	0	0	0	−1	−1	−1
5	1	0	0	−1	−1	−1
6	1	1	1	−1	−1	−1

In this example three content specialists have been asked to match six items to two objectives. Items 1–3 "ideally" match objective 1 and items 4–6 "ideally" match objective 2. The computation of I_{ik} for the match between item 1 and objective 1 is as follows:

$I_{11} = [(N-1) (G_1) - (H) + (G_1)]/[2(N-1)n]$
$I_{11} = [(2-1) (3) - (0) + (3)]/[2(2-1)3]$
$I_{11} = 1$
where:
$N = 2$
$G_1 = 1 + 1 + 1 = 3$
$H = 1 + 1 + 1 - 1 - 1 - 1 = 0$
$n = 3$

The computation of I_{ik} for the match of items 2 and 3 to their assigned objective are:

Item 2;
$I_{21} = [(2-1) (2) - (0) + 2]/6 = .67$
Item 3;
$I_{31} = [(2-1) (0) - (0) + 0]/6 = .00$
Similarly, I_{ik} for items 4–6 is:
Item 4;
$I_{42} = [(2-1) (-3) - (-3) + (-3)]/6 = -.50$
Item 5;
$I_{52} = [(2-1) (-3) - (-2) + (-3)]/6 = -.67$
Item 6;
$I_{62} = [(2-1) (-3) - (0) + (-3)]/6 = -1$

Summarizing:	Item	I_{ik}
	1	1.00
	2	.67
	3	.00
	4	−.50
	5	−.67
	6	−1.00

The *Index* for item 1 suggests a high level of congruence between the item and the objective with which it is associated. When one examines the ratings given the item by the content specialists, this congruence indeed becomes clear; each specialist rated the item as definitely matching objective 1 and definitely not matching any other objective. The opposite is true for item 6, which has an *Index* of −1.00. The ratings support this as the specialists unanimously rejected the item as matching the "proper" objective (2) and rated it as matching the "wrong" objective (1).

Once the *Index of Item-Objective Congruence* has been determined, a judgment must be made about what separates a "good" item from a "bad" item. There is no statistical test which can be applied that would ease this dilemma. Hambleton (1977) suggests that the professional staff create a situation which represents the minimum set of ratings which would be considered for retention of an item, compute the *Index*, and use it as the decision-point for item inclusion.

Part B

Table 7.
Item Difficulty Estimates, and Associated Statistics for Two Competencies, IOX Basic Skill Test Reading; Forms A and B

Competency 2		Competency 3	
Form A	*Form B*	*Form A*	*Form B*
.989	−.434	.014	−1.805
−.023	−1.217	−1.829	1.551
1.114	−1.469	−.827	−1.467
−.588	−.446	−.544	1.265
−.684	−1.766	−1.289	−.782
$\bar{X}=.162$	−1.066	−.895	−.248
$S^2=.726$	.366	1.296	2.490

note: The item difficulty estimates are d-values, which range (increasing) from approximately −5 to +5 (Wright and Stone, 1979).

The data presented in Table 7 appear to support the supposition that, when test forms are not properly equated, low reliability may be due to differences in the difficulty (and variance) of the items.

As a hypothetical situation, if Form A had been administered to this year's sophomore class and Form B had been administered to the sophomore class the following year, erroneous generalizations about the comparative performance of the classes over time may be made (assuming the distribution of achievement for the two classes is approximately equivalent). This is true particularly in the absence of reliability and item difficulty information of the type presented above.

Index

Ginnie Rhodes Nuta, Production Editor
Glenna F. Bergquist, Indexer